T0339677

MEDINA MAYRIT

MEDINA MAYRIT

THE ORIGINS OF MADRID

ANA RUIZ

Algora Publishing
New York

Library of Congress Cataloging-in-Publication Data —

Ruiz, Ana.
  Medina Mayrit: the origins of Madrid / Ana Ruiz.
    p. cm.
  Includes bibliographical references and index.
  ISBN 978-0-87586-924-7 (soft cover: alk. paper)—ISBN 978-0-87586-925-4
(hard cover: alk. paper)—ISBN 978-0-87586-926-1 (ebook) 1. Madrid (Spain)—
History. 2. Madrid (Spain)—Description and travel. I. Title.
  DP354.R85 2012
  946'.41—dc23
                           2012001695

Front Cover: Old Madrid, painting by Manuel Ruiz (1920–2010)

Printed in the United States

To my father, Manuel Ruiz (1920–2010), who inspired my interest with his extensive knowledge about the origins of our birthplace.

TABLE OF CONTENTS

FOREWORD

Founded during the 9th century, Madrid is one of the few settlements in Muslim Spain or al-Andalus that was entirely created by the Moors—unlike cities that were built upon former Roman or Visigoth sites, such as Toledo and Córdoba. *Medina Mayrit* translates as "City of Madrid" in the Arabic language and exclusively refers to the Moorish era of the city.

Prior to the arrival of the Muslims this, the future capital of the country, was inhabited by Celt-Iberians, Romans, and Visigoths; however, it remained a modest rural village of farmers and peasants until the Moors conquered most of the Iberian Peninsula (Spain and Portugal). Explored here are the prehistoric beginnings of Madrid through to its early Christian period. The remnants of Moorish Madrid that are still visible today are discussed, while an entire chapter is devoted to the city of Toledo, as Mayrit belonged to its Taifa Kingdom. Also incorporated are interesting and curious facts about Madrid for history buffs and travelers as well as etymological theories regarding the origins of many Castilian place-names and terms appearing throughout this work.

As dates may differ according to sources, and variations of spelling also exist, I have chosen what I believe to be most accurate.

Terms have been translated to the best of my linguistic abilities, and the photographs were taken on my own numerous trips, unless otherwise specified — such as those taken by my father, Manuel Ruiz, fellow native of Madrid, who is also the gifted artist behind the artwork.

Compared to other major cities of al-Andalus, little has been written about Madrid during its Muslim era, particularly in the English language. Therefore, I wish to share my studies as an introduction to the Moorish origins and history of my birthplace of Madrid, the capital of the Kingdom of Spain.

Ana Ruiz
Montreal, 2012

Muslim Timeline of the Iberian Peninsula (710–1492)

710 – Tarif ibn Malik disembarks at Tarifa

711 – Tariq ibn Ziyad disembarks at Gibraltar

  – Battle of Guadalete

  – Umayyad Caliphate establishes Seville as capital of al-Andalus

712 – Musa ibn Nusayr disembarks at Algecíras

716 – Córdoba replaces Seville as the Umayyad capital of al-Andalus

722 – Christian victory over the Moors at the Battle of Covadonga

732 – Frankish victory over the Moors at the Battle of Poitiers

755 – Abd ar-Rahman I disembarks at Almuñécar

756 – Abd ar-Rahman I proclaims himself Emir establishing the independent Umayyad Emirate of Córdoba

788 – Death of Abd ar-Rahman I

822 – Muhammad I is born

852 – Muhammad I becomes Emir of Córdoba

854 – Moorish victory over the Christians at the Battle of Guadelete

865 – Approximate year that Mayrit is founded by Muhammad I

886 – Death of Emir Muhammad I

924 – Fernán González unsuccessfully attempts to conquer Mayrit

929 – Abd ar-Rahman III proclaims himself Caliph establishing the independent Umayyad Caliphate of Córdoba

932 – Alcázar of Mayrit is destroyed by Christians under King Ramiro II of León

939 – Ramiro II defeats Abd ar-Rahman III at the Battle of Simancas

940 – Madrid recaptured and rebuilt by Abd ar-Rahman III

950 – Al-Mayriti is born

– Mayrit is attacked by Ramiro II and Fernán Gonzalez

1035 – Umayyad Caliphate Era of Córdoba ends and Taifa Period begins

– Approximate date that Mayrit is incorporated into Taifa of Toledo

1047 – Mayrit is temporarily conquered by King Fernando I King of Castile

1085 – Mayrit and Toledo are permanently conquered by Christians

1109 – Unsuccessful siege by Almorávide Ali ibn Yusuf at Campo del Moro

1147 – The Almohades overthrow the Almorávides

1198 – Unsuccessful siege by Almohad Abu Yusuf Ya'qub al-Mansur at Campo del Moro

1202 – Madrid is granted official status of town by Alfonso VIII

1212 – Almohades defeated at the battle of Las Navas de Tolosa

1232 – Nasrid Kingdom of Granada is established as last Muslim stronghold in Spain

1492 – Granada is conquered by the Catholic Kings

1. MANTUA CARPETANA — ANCIENT MADRID

Although the capital of Spain was founded by the Moors as a fortress during the second half of the 9th century, archaeological evidence reveals habitation in this region since prehistoric times. A variety of stone tools, artifacts, weapons and hunting tools, as well as animal remains, have been excavated in the terrace deposits along the Manzanares, Jarama, and Henares Rivers that surround the region of Madrid.

The oldest human remains in the province were discovered within the archaeological zone and small municipality northeast of Madrid known as Pinilla de Valle in the Lozoya Valley, and they have been dated prior to the existence of *Homo neanderthals* who entered the peninsula through the Pyrenees Mountains. Excavations in this area since this accidental discovery in 1979 have yielded a wealth of information in the forms of animal and human remains as well as stone tools and weapons dated to the Lower Paleolithic Era.

About 350,000 years ago, settlers began to inhabit the region of the Manzanares Valley by the river due to its abundance of natural resources and steady flow of water supply. Horses, elephants, mammoths, bulls, rhinoceroses, hippopotamuses, and deer all drank from the Manzanares River with its many streams and brooks.

The first and most significant archaeological discovery began in 1862 in what are known as the *Manzanares Terraces* or deposits along the margins of the Manzanares River. Over the years, remains of fossilized animals dated to the Paleolithic Era have been excavated. These animal remains stand as the oldest of their kind to be found in the country. Also discovered were an abundance of material such as well-preserved carved flint stones, tools, arrows, pots, bracelets, weapons, and various other artifacts.

At the *Museo de Orígenes* (Museum of Origins) at Plaza San Andrés in the historic section of Madrid, hunting tools are displayed from 500,000 years ago. Also exhibited is an extensive archaeological collection that includes gold jewelry, fine ceramics, the remains of ancient mammals, as well as a molar from a young boy found in the area that are all dated to the Paleolithic Era.

In 1976, further excavations performed in Arganda del Rey of the Jarama Valley revealed further significant archaeological findings that were dated to the Middle Pleistocene Age. These sites were named Áridos I and Áridos II. At Áridos I, along with pieces of flint and quartzite tools were the scattered remains of a straight-tusked, adult female elephant; the partial skeleton of a male elephant was unearthed at the nearby and less well-preserved site of Áridos II, dated to the Middle Pleistocene Age.

The Iberians

The Iberians were the first known inhabitants of the peninsula; they were named by the Greeks after the longest and most important river in the country, the *Iber* or Ebro River. Although there are several theories regarding their origins, many believe that the Iberians arrived from the eastern Mediterranean region of Asia Minor with roots going back over 5,000 years. These tribes appear to have migrated to Spain during the 3rd or perhaps the 4th millennium BCE. Another theory claims that the Iberians migrated from Western or Eastern Europe while others insist that they came from North Africa during the Neolithic period.

It is generally believed that the Iberians are the direct ancestors of the Basques. This theory is backed up by ancient Iberian coins that display names of places that are still in use today in addition to the similarities between the Iberian and Basque languages.

Dama de Elche

The Iberians settled in the region between the northern area of the hill where the royal palace of Madrid stands today down to Las Vistillas in the south. These people were skilled in agricultural techniques as they cultivated land while raising sheep, pigs, and cattle. They were hardworking and resourceful, possessing considerable knowledge in metallurgy and eventually trading precious metals with the Phoenicians, Greeks, and Carthaginians while living in their isolated communities. Fine Iberian ceramics and artwork have been discovered as far away as North Africa, France, and Italy. The most outstanding example is the limestone bust of a woman known as the *Dama de Elche* or "Lady of Elche." The figure of a woman (or perhaps priestess) has been named after the eastern town of Elche in the province of Alicante where it was discovered in 1897. This unique sculpture is considered to be a masterpiece of Iberian art. The face of the mysterious woman displays a slightly commanding expression yet at the same time she seems almost to be in some sort of trance or deep thought. She is adorned by an elaborate circular ceremonial headdress as well as heavy ear pieces and several detailed necklaces that drape across her front. She may have been a funerary or fertility goddess, as her hollowed-out back was likely used to hold offerings, religious objects, or funerary ashes. The sculpture, dated to the 5th or 4th century BCE, is presently on display at the National Archaeological Museum of Madrid.

The Celts

Around 1100 BCE, Phoenician settlers established an important colony in the south of Spain, known as *Gades* or Cádiz, that is considered to be the oldest town in Western Europe. From the 10th to 7th centuries BCE, Celtic tribes of Indo-European origin migrated in waves from Eastern Europe and merged with the existing Iberians, forming the *Celtiberian* tribe that settled in the Ebro Valley, spreading to the eastern coast of the *Levante*. The first Celtiberian settlements in the area of Madrid were established between the Jarama River and the Guadarrama River, or Manzanares River as it is known since the 17th century.

The Celtiberian tribes that settled in this valley are known as the *Carpetanos* or *Carpetani*; they lived in the region of *Carpetania* that extended from the Guadarrama Sierra to the Tagus River or *Rio Tajo*. The land of the Carpetanos included not only Madrid but Cuenca, part of Ciudad Real, and Guadalajara, as well as nearly the entire province of Toledo.

Carpetania was a fertile land rich in fruits and as the Carpetanos were a combination of skilled shepherds and farmers, they dedicated themselves to agriculture and the cultivation of vegetables and barley. These tribes also raised livestock for wool and milk, and they excelled in metalwork as well.

The capital of Carpetania was *Mantua Carpetana*, the location of which today remains somewhat undetermined. One theory is that it was located where the present-day suburb of *Mostoles* is found. In the *Tables of Ptolemy* (2nd century ADE), it is stated that Mantua Carpetana was situated at the center of the peninsula in the region of Talamanca. Others, however, theorize that it was in Villamanta, where many vestiges dated to the Roman period have been excavated. According to both Ptolemy (c. 90–170 ADE) and Pliny the Elder (23–79 ADE), the Carpetanos settled in *Complutum* (Alcalá de

Henares), *Miacum* (Casa de Campo), *Toletum* (Toledo), and *Titulcia* (a location that also has not precisely been determined).

During the 6th century BCE, Greek explorers began entering the Iberian Peninsula and established a trading colony along the Mediterranean Coast in *Emporium*, known today as *Ampurias*. The Greeks were followed by the Carthaginians, about a century after, who were descendants of the Phoenicians. The Carthaginians also established their capital along the Mediterranean coast in *Cartagena* while driving out the Greek settlers, remaining here for nearly three centuries.

Until as recent as the 19th century of our era, scholars believed that Madrid was actually founded by the Greeks and Romans, but no archaeological proof or document has ever corroborated this theory. It does, however, survive in the form of a legend...

The Legend of Prince Ocnus

According to Greek and Roman mythology, King *Tyrrhenius* of Tuscany had a child with a woman named *Mantua* who was a fortune-teller. Mantua was the daughter of *Tyresia*, the blind prophet from the Greek city of Thebes. In order to escape the tribulations of illegitimacy, the king bestowed Mantua and her little prince with many riches and sent them away to live in northern Italy.

When the young prince came of age, he re-established the Etruscan city of *Manto*, known today as *Mántova*, in northern Italy. However, it was not long before he found himself haunted and greatly disturbed by a prophetic dream. In this dream, the great god Apollo himself appeared and advised the young prince to decline rulership of the kingdom that he would soon come to inherit upon his mother's death. Instead, the prince was instructed to seek and establish a new kingdom: otherwise a great epidemic would devastate the inhabitants and the town of Manto.

From this day forth, the young prince was known as *Ocnus Bianor*, named after his grandfather *Prince Bianor*, in reference to his ability to "see" the future in his dreams (*oculus* is Latin for "eye" and the suffix "us" implies ownership). Ocnus made his decision and departed for the land of Spain, where he dwelled in caves for a decade until one night when once again the mighty Apollo appeared to him in a dream. This time the great god informed Ocnus that he had finally arrived at his chosen destiny, where he was instructed to build a new city and kingdom. However, there was one stipulation—Ocnus must sacrifice his own life for this new kingdom in order to ensure faith in his followers.

Upon awakening from this disturbing dream, Ocnus realized that he was humbled before a bountiful land that was rich in vegetation and forest, with an abundance of madrone trees as well as a steady supply of water. Here, he encountered the small population of Carpetanos who had been patiently waiting for a sign from their gods as to where to establish their permanent homeland.

Ocnus related his dream to the Carpetanos, who were somewhat distrustful, fearing that this stranger wanted to take possession of the land for himself. He had no alternative, and as proof of his nobility, sincerity, and loyalty, Ocnus declared to the Carpetanos that he would sacrifice his own life for this new kingdom.

The Carpetanos accepted his offer and began to construct a small city with a palace, several houses, and a temple for worshipping. Ocnus named the land *Mantua* after his mother and *Carpetana* after its inhabitants (in order to differentiate it from the other Mantua, in Italy). Mantua Carpetana became the most important colony of the Carpetanos.

The new town of Mantua was consecrated to the goddess *Metragirta* (or Cybele), daughter of Saturn, who was also known as the *Mother of the Gods* and the *Great Mother*. The cult of Cybele goes as far back as 1200 BCE when she was worshipped in Asia Minor as the Phrygian goddess of fertility. Today, Cybele is immortalized as a magnificent sculpture in the centerpiece of the late 18th century fountain at the *Plaza de Cibeles* in downtown Madrid. The sculpture of the goddess in a royal chariot being pulled along by two lions has become one of the city's most emblematic symbols.

Once the town was built, Ocnus requested his own burial, to the reluctance of the Carpetanos, who obeyed their founder's wishes and mourned their savior. Shortly afterwards, a horrible storm took place, one so severe its likes had never been seen before. Suddenly, a massive cloud appeared in the thunderous sky in the shape of Metragirta riding upon her celestial chariot while carrying the body of Ocnus up to the heavens. By sunrise, the land was once again calm and the grave of Ocnus had all but vanished, leaving behind a trail of flowers.

La Cibeles

Pedro Texeira (1595–1662) was a Portuguese explorer, geographer, and cartographer who died in Madrid. In the year 1656, Texeira composed a map of medieval Madrid that is considered as the most significant of its kind. The map is carries the following Latin inscription:

> MANTVA, CARPETANORVM, SIVE MATRITVM VRBS REGIA
>
> (MANTUA, CARPETANORUM, OR MATRITUM ROYAL CITY)

Mantua Carpetana was founded over a century earlier than Rome. An anonymous Jesuit priest wrote a sonata during the 17th century in the voice of Mantua Carpetana:

> ...Soy *más [sic] que Roma Antigua, buen testigo es el rey Ocnus,*
> *y de su madre el nombre.*
> ...I am more [old] than ancient Rome, fine witness is king Ocnus, and from his mother [is] the name.

But when the mighty Romans came, the Carpetanos were no match for them and the Romans conquered the Iberian Peninsula for themselves. By 133 BCE, the Romans completed their mission and what followed were six centuries of Roman rule in Spain.

2. MATRICE (ROMAN AND VISIGOTH MADRID)

When the Romans arrived at what we know today as Madrid, they encountered a small rural area along the Manzanares River inhabited by the Carpetanos. The Celtiberian tribe did offer some resistance; however, the Romans were interested in this central region for its strategic position and they took it by force. Here, they established a small settlement by the Manzanares River during the 2nd century BCE and named it *Matrice*, meaning "mother of waters," in reference to the stream that then ran along present-day Segovia Street.

Spain was valued by the Romans primarily because of the numerous gold, silver, iron, copper, and lead mines in the area. The Romans also had their eyes on the Celts, who were fearless warriors that were easily recruited for the Roman Army. Spain provided Rome with three emperors: Trajan (53–117 ADE), Hadrian (76–138 ADE), and Theodosius (347–395 ADE), all born at Italica, about 7 miles from the city of Seville in present-day Santiponce.

The Romans invaded the land in 206 BCE, but it took nearly two centuries for the Iberian Peninsula to be fully Romanized. They named their territory *Hispania*, from which the name of Spain is derived. During their 600-year rule in the Iberian Peninsula, the

Romans introduced the Latin language that formed the basis of Castilian (Spanish) language. These conquerors also laid the foundations for the country's legal system, administrative and government structure, as well as the religion by introducing Christianity. Public work projects were realized through trading such valuable commodities as oil, wine, cereal, and metals. The Romans also built networks of roads that were used for military and commercial or trade purposes in addition to building magnificent structures and monuments including bridges, amphitheaters, and aqueducts throughout the land.

About 56 miles north of Madrid lies the enchanting town of Segovia, where the most impressive Roman site can be admired in the form of a splendid aqueduct that is dated between the 1st and 2nd century ADE. Situated in the center of the city, the aqueduct was used to transport water from the *Fuenfría Spring* or *Riofrío* (Cold River) that flowed from the mountains in the region of *Acebeda* about 12 miles away. This remarkable example of ancient architecture, still in use until the mid 20th century, is comprised of 20, 400 granite blocks that are secured only by gravity; it was built without mortar or cement.

Aqueduct

Still standing after two millennia, this magnificent structure is considered to be the best preserved example of Roman civil engineering in the world.

Hispania

Hispania was divided into two regions, Hispania Citerior (Nearer Spain) to the east, and Hispania Ulterior (Farther Spain) to the south. In 71 BCE, Julius Caesar was named Governor of Hispania Ulterior and in 27 BCE his grand nephew became Emperor Augustus (63 BCE–14 ADE). The Emperor renamed most of Hispania Ulterior as *Baética* after the *Guadalquivir* River or *Baetis*, as it was then known, that flowed through the region. *Córduba* (Córdoba) was selected as the capital of Baética, which corresponds with most of the southern region of Andalusia today.

Within Hispania Citerior were two main cities: *Complutum* and *Toletum*. Complutum, situated on the banks of the Henares River and known today as Alcalá de Henares, was the only settlement in the area that was mentioned by Roman geographers of the 1st century ADE. By the time the Romans arrived, Toletum (Toledo) was already a well-defended settlement, situated upon a hilltop overlooking the plains, surrounded and protected on three sides by the Tagus River and Gorge. Roman historian Titus Livius (59 BCE–17 ADE) was the first to write about Toledo, which became a Roman municipality in 192 BCE:

> *Toletum, ibi parva urbis erat, sed loco munito.*

> Toledo, a small city, but strong due to its location.

Traversing Hispania, the Romans constructed a commercial road that measured about 932 miles in length. Emperor Augustus named the *Vía Augusta* after himself as he was responsible for the repair and renovation of this significant roadway between the years 8 and 2 BCE. The Vía Augusta was the chief commercial route of transportation and a vital trade link between the major cities and ports within the country. The route extended from Rome to Gades (Cádiz), passing through the cities of *Carthago Nova* (Cartagena)

, *Valentia* (Valencia), *Tarraco* (Tarragona), *Gerunda* (Gerona), and *Barcino* (Barcelona.)

The region of Madrid was located at the intersection of important roadways that passed through the Iberian Peninsula. These two main roadways were offshoots of the Vía Augusta that linked *Caesar-Augusta* (Zaragoza) with *Emérita-Augusta* (Mérida) while passing through Toletum and the roadway linking *Astúrica* (Astorga) with Córduba. It was in *Titulcia* that the intersection of these and other minor roads met.

Titulcia, mentioned by Ptolemy in his *Geography*, remains undiscovered and is not believed to have been located where the municipality named Titulcia is situated today. Some historians state that ancient Titulcia was located just over a mile north of the town of *Aranjuez* that lies south of Madrid.

The largest Roman urban settlements in the area after Toletum and Complutum were Titulcia and *Miacum*, by the *Meaques* Stream of the Manzanares River, by Casa de Campo in Madrid. Like Titulcia, historians do not agree on where ancient Miacum was located; however, it is generally believed that it was situated where *Las Rozas* is today. Historian *Antonio Caracalla*, who lived during the 3rd century of our era, designed a map of Roman routes of the Iberian Peninsula; this map is known as *Itinerario Antonino* (Itinerary of Antonino). In his itinerary he cites Miacum, a small Roman settlement, as one of the "mansions" where one could stop to rest on the route that linked Titulcia with Segovia.

From Roman Madrid, vestiges in the form of memorial tablets inscribed in Latin as well as mosaics that once adorned luxurious villas have been discovered. These large Roman villas, mainly of a farming or agricultural nature, were generally built near the communication routes, close to the river but on elevated ground to avoid flooding, and close to forests where firewood was available and hunting opportunities were abundant. Most of the Roman villas were permanently abandoned by the 5th century; traces of some of these villas have been found in the areas of Madrid at Casa de Campo, Villaverde Bajo, Carabanchel, Jarama-Henares, El Val, Getafe, La Torrecilla, Barajas, and Quatro Caminos. These ruins demonstrate that Roman Madrid was not an urban nucleus but rather an area of cultivated farmland and rural estates. Large fragments of mosaics from the Roman Villas of Carabanchel (3rd century) and Villaverde Bajo (1st century) are currently displayed at Madrid's Museo de Orígenes. The collection also includes luxurious objects from the Villaverde Bajo villa in the form of imported stained glass, stone and bronze sculptures, ceramics, detailed plates, dishes, and bronze coins dated to the 1st and 2nd centuries ADE. Additional Roman treasures on display include iron weapons, fine jewelry, ceramic jars of all shapes, alabaster urns, silver coins, sarcophagi, marble statues, and bronze chandeliers.

The Germanic Invasion

During the 3rd century, a Germanic tribe known as the Goths separated into two groups; the East Goths or *Ostrogoths* established themselves in Italy and the West Goths or *Visigoths* settled in southwestern France with their capital in Toulouse.

In the year 409 ADE, barbarian tribes such as the *Vandals* and *Sueves* of East Germany, along with the *Alans* (or Alani) of East Iran, began entering the Iberian Peninsula through the Pyrenees Mountains from Catalonia. As the Roman Empire began to collapse, assistance was requested from the powerful Visigoths in driving out the Vandals, Sueves, and Alans from the country.

It was the year 456 when *Theodoric II*, King of the Visigoths, entered Hispania and defeated the Sueves, dethroning King *Rechiarius* of Galicia. By 476 ADE the Visigoth conquest of Spain was complete. In the year 507, after losing his capital of Toulouse to the Franks, Visigoth ruler of Hispania *Leovigild* (r. 569–586) established the capital in Toledo. Roman Spain became history.

What the **Visigoths contributed to Spain was** a centralized government, new laws, and a reasonable tax system. The Visigoths adopted Christianity and maintained the name of Matrice (pronounced "matriche") that the Romans had established. The Visigoths were few in number and mainly occupied abandoned Roman villas, while establishing a few villages of their own.

The remains of a Visigoth necropolis are also on display at the Museo de Orígenes; it was situated at *Daganzo de Arriba* in Madrid. This necropolis was discovered in 1929 when an accident involving a wagon unearthed tracings of a cemetery containing over 50 graves, including a pantheon belonging to a noble 6th century family of five that were laid to rest in wooden coffins. Included in their funerary remains was a sword with a rich sheath decorated in silver belonging to the young boy of the family.

Remains of another Visigoth necropolis have been discovered in the area of Madrid near Casa de Campo; in the burial sites relics such as a broach, belt buckles, and various metallic objects have been unearthed. In the district of *Tetuán de las Victorias*, vestiges of another Visigoth cemetery have been revealed including a bronze belt buckle that is currently displayed at the Archaeological Museum of Madrid.

Very little has been discovered regarding Visigoth Madrid and some experts even dispute that it ever existed, as there is no evidence in either documents or architecture. Most, however, agree that between the 7th and 8th centuries there very well could have been a small Visigoth settlement in *Matrice* on the banks of the San Pedro stream that ran down today's Segovia Street across Cerro de las Vistillas. Regardless, it is most likely that the Visigoth settlement never grew beyond a quite small, rural, and primitive village with inhabitants dedicated to farming, hunting, and fishing, and never reaching any great significance in urban status.

Further testimony of a Visigoth population existing in Madrid lies in a badly deteriorated memorial tablet found with a Latin inscription bearing the era 738 that corresponds to 700 ADE. The tablet, never fully translated to the satisfaction of historians, was discovered in 1618 inside the cloister of what once was the Church of Santa María on the corner of *Mayor* and *Bailén* streets in old Madrid. However, skeptics are quick to point out that the tablet could have been transported from another area. Although it is lost through the centuries, historical records tell us that it bore the following inscription:

IN NNE DOMINI BOKATVS INDIGNVS PRSBTR OBIT AN

NO TERTIO DECIMO ET TERTIO REGNO DOMNORVM EGICANI ET

WITTIZAN RGVM ERA DCCXXXVIII

In the name of the Lord, [a] local man of religious vocation dies in the 13th and 3rd year of reign of our rulers Egica and Witiza in the year 738.

Egica and *Witiza* were Visigoth kings of Hispania. Egica (r. 687–702) was known to be a cruel man, particularly to the Jewish population as he implemented harsher anti-Jewish laws than any other Visigoth ruler. These included the forfeit of their land and the prohibition of passing on the teachings of the Torah to children. The Jewish population could not build new synagogues or own properties, nor were they permitted to engage in business transactions with Christians.

Egica had a son named Witiza (r. 702–710), whom he named as co-regent. Witiza was regarded as a more humane ruler; he did not impose further strict conditions against the Jewish population, but he did not eradicate them, either. Witiza started out as a responsible ruler, then gave into his many desires and self-indulgences while encouraging others to do likewise. Before Witiza died, he appointed his son *Akhila* as successor. However, the nobility rejected Akhila, preferring a commander named *Rodrigo* (r. 710–711) to take his place upon the Visigoth throne.

It could very well be that a humiliated and defeated Akhila and his followers formed an alliance with the Moors and called upon their help in exacting revenge, thus instigating the Muslim invasion of the Iberian Peninsula. There is little doubt that the Visigoths planned the conquest, and it seems likely that they foolishly expected the Moors to return to their land once Rodrigo was defeated.

Another plausible theory is that the Jewish population that had inhabited the land since the Roman Era, excelling as translators, scholars, well-respected merchants, and money-lenders, welcomed the new conquerors and may have been instrumental in overthrowing the anti-Jewish Visigoths.

According to legend, when Rodrigo was placed in power he came upon the knowledge of a secret treasure of riches and wisdom that had been locked away for centuries inside a cave in Toledo. It was customary for a newly-installed king to place a sturdy lock upon the gate of this cave. Hercules himself, as the legend goes, placed the very first lock. The king soon learned that anyone who had tried to break the locks in the past had been cursed, meeting unfortunate circumstances. Rodrigo was to add the 27th lock; however, his curiosity overpowered his fear. The invincible ruler was quite intrigued by the story of the hidden treasure, shrugged off the warnings, and assembled a group of soldiers to assist in breaking all the locks so he could obtain the riches.

Entering the cavern, Rodrigo ignored the curses that were inscribed upon the walls; however, he was soon horrified at what he saw. Upon a wall in the darkened corridor appeared the vivid image of hundreds of armed soldiers of darker skin mounted upon horses, dressed in colorful garb, with turbans on their heads and swords and spears in hand. King Rodrigo and his men immediately shut the gates and fled the cave in terror. It was only a few weeks later that the prophecy came to pass, as Rodrigo, the last Visigoth king of Hispania, was defeated by the Moors at the Battle of Guadalete in July of 711.

Although Rodrigo is regarded as the last Visigoth ruler in Spain, it is more accurate to say that he was the last ruler of Visigoth Spain. After the Moors conquered the land in 711, *Akhila II* succeeded Rodrigo and ruled what little remained of the former Visigoth Hispania, the Roman province of *Tarraconensis* in Hispania Citerior. His rule during Moorish Spain was brief as he died in 714.

I close this chapter with another interesting legend involving the weaknesses of King Rodrigo and the loss of Visigoth Spain.

The Legend and Ballad of King Rodrigo

Rodrigo, who ruled from Toledo, was a red-blooded man of basic desires that he found difficult to control. Characteristically, his temptation ruled over logic and each afternoon the king secretly watched as a beautiful maiden bathed while he hid behind a thick bush. This young beauty was no simple maiden; she was *Florinda*, the youngest daughter of Count Julian, governor of Ceuta and Algeciras. Florinda (also known as *La Cava* in Muslim chronicles; that translates to something synonymous to "the seductress") had been sent to Toledo to receive a good education. It was traditional for those of better means to send their daughters and sons to study in the Visigoth capital.

The day arrived when King Rodrigo could no longer resist temptation while he admired Florinda bathing, and he went forth and took advantage of her. When Don Julian learned of the incident, he became furious and called upon his fellow Muslims to help him take revenge; indeed, they had already had their eyes on southern Spain. And help him they did, as they arrived in the south of the Iberian Peninsula in the year 712, with Governor and General *Musa ibn Nusayr* at the head of an army of 16,000 soldiers.

Today the tower where the lovely Florinda bathed is named in her honor: *Baño de la Cava* (Bath of the Cava). I leave it up to my readers to draw their own conclusions, whether the legend is partly based on facts, or the reverse—could the Moorish invasion of Spain perhaps have been triggered by a scorned woman seeking revenge? Or did the king use his daughter's misfortune as a catalyst to galvanize the forces needed to conquer the land?

Baño de la Cava

During the 15th century, an anonymous form of poetry known as Romance literature became quite popular. These special forms of verse compositions covered a variety of subjects and were so named because they were written in the Romance dialect of the Latin language. The following is a sample of Romance literature titled *The Ballad of Cava Florinda and King Rodrigo*:

De una torre de Palacio
se salió por un postigo,
la Cava con sus doncellas
con gran fiesta y regocijo.

Reposaron las doncellas
buscando solaz y alivio
al fuego de mocedad
y a los ardores de estío

Daban al agua sus brazos,
y tentada de su frió,
fue la Cava la primera
que desnudó sus vestidos.

En la sombreada alberca
su cuerpo brilla tan lindo
que al de todas las demás
como sol ha oscurecido.

Pensó la Cava estar sola,
pero la venturo quiso
que entre unas espesas yedras
la miraba el rey Rodrigo.

Puso la ocasión el fuego
en el corazón altivo,
y el amor, batiendo sus alas,
abrasóle de improviso.

De la perdida de España
fue aquí funesto principio
una mujer sin ventura
y un hombre de amor rendido.

Florinda perdió su flor,
el rey padeció el castigo;
ella dice que hubo fuerza,
el que gusto consentido.

Si dicen quien de los dos
la mayor culpa ha tenido,
digan los hombres: La Cava
y las mujeres: Rodrigo.

From a tower of the palace
emerging from a secret door,
came La Cava with her girlfriends
seeking fun and nothing more...

...The maidens took their ease
searching solace and relief
from the fires of their youth
and the warmth of summer's heat.

Giving their arms to the water,
and feeling its cool caress,
La Cava was the first
to remove her clothes, and undress.

In the shaded pond
her glistening body was so fair,
the other maidens
were dimmed, beyond compare.

La Cava thought she was alone,
but as fate decreed,
watching her was King Rodrigo
behind a leafy tree.

He took advantage of the fire
within his arrogant heart,
and love, fluttering its wings,
suddenly burned apart.

The loss of Spain
began in that ill-fated start
a woman with no luck
and a king overcome by his heart.

Florinda lost her honor,
the king endured his punishment;
she says there was force,
he, that it was mutual consent.

If asked to which of them
the blame should go,
men say: La Cava
and women: Rodrigo.

3. Mayrit, 8ᵀᴴ–9ᵀᴴ Centuries

A rapid expansion of the Islamic faith followed the death of the Prophet Muhammad in 632 ADE. In less than a century, Islam had spread to span all of North Africa, the Middle East, and all the way to Pakistan. From Morocco, the Muslims entered the Iberian Peninsula and by the late 8ᵗʰ century they occupied most of the land, excluding certain mountainous regions in the north. The debilitated and crumbling Visigoth kingdom could not defeat the mighty Moors who conquered most of the land, becoming well established throughout the Iberian Peninsula. The new conquerors named this land *al-Andalus*. This was Moorish Spain.

In July of 710, the Moors arrived at Tarifa in the province of *Qadis* (Cádiz) at the southernmost tip of Spain. Tarifa is named after the Berber officer and general *Tarif ibn Malik* (born *Abu Zar'a Tarif ibn Malik al-Ma'afiri*), who headed the mission, accompanied by 500 men. The following April, a far larger expedition was dispatched of 7,000 to 12,000 soldiers who were mostly comprised of Berber troops from North Africa along with 300 Syrian Arabs.

Tarifa

Gibraltar

In 711 Muslim governor of North Africa, *Musa ibn Nusayr* (640–716 ADE), sent for his best man, a Berber general and lieutenant of Tangiers named *Tariq ibn Ziyad*, known as *El Tuerto* (The One-

Eyed). The lieutenant arrived at the Iberian Peninsula with an army of 16,000 men comprised of Berbers from Morocco and Arabs from Tunisia, Algiers, and Libya. Tariq, a member of the *Nafza* tribe of North Africa, disembarked at the site in 711 that was to bear his name: Gibraltar (derived from *Gebel al-Tariq* or "Tariq's Mountain").

The *Umayyad* Dynasty or *Banu Umayyah* (family or children of Umayyah) from Damascus claimed to be direct descendants of the prophet Muhammad through a common ancestor from Mecca. The son of this ancestor, *Umayyah ibn Abd Shams*, was the father of the Caliph *Mu'awiya* who founded this Islamic dynasty in 661. The Umayyads ruled what was then the largest empire of the world as the first Islamic Caliphate that lasted until 750.

In the summer of 712, Governor Musa ibn Nusayr led an additional expedition of 18,000 soldiers. The governor, accompanied by his eldest son *Abd al-aziz ibn Musa ibn Nusayr*, departed from *Medina Sebta* (Ceuta, a Spanish enclave in North Africa) and disembarked at *al-Jazirah al-Khadra* ("the Green Island," otherwise known as Algeciras) in the province of Cádiz. Shortly afterwards, Musa was summoned back to Damascus by the Umayyad Caliphate, and he left his son, *Abd al-Aziz*, in charge, to govern in his name.

In the year 713, Abd al-Aziz signed a treaty with Visigoth commander *Theodemir* of the eastern region of Murcia and Alicante. This pact permitted, after some resistance, the Visigoths to maintain their religion by paying a small tribute. This peaceful agreement, known as the *Treaty of Tudmir*, formed just two years after the Moorish conquest of the peninsula, indicates that the Muslims maintained a somewhat tolerant and diplomatic disposition towards the Christian Visigoths.

Tariq ibn Ziyad and Musa ibn Nusayr, respectively, were the first governors of al-Andalus; however, neither resided in the Iberian Peninsula. In the year 713/714, Abd al-Aziz made *Ishbiliyah* (Seville) his capital and became the first governor of al-Andalus to actually rule from the newly conquered land. Abd al-Aziz married a beautiful Christian woman named *Egilona Egitania*, who was also known as *Ailo* by the Muslims. Egilona happened to be the widow of Rodrigo, the last King of Visigoth Spain.

Abd al-Aziz settled in Seville with his new wife, who converted to Islam. However, as a former Christian, Egilona persuaded Abd al-Aziz to show some mercy to the Christian prisoners, and this did not sit well with the Caliphate of Damascus. The Visigoth widow went so far as to convince Abd al-Aziz to wear a crown; "A king has no kingdom if he wears no crown," Egilona told her husband. She offered to create a crown for him, fashioned from her precious jewels and gold pieces. He resisted, she persisted, and he finally complied.

Abd al-Aziz wore a crown behind closed doors until he was seen by a female relative. As expected, his secret was exposed and fuel had been added to the spark created when he married a Christian woman. Egilona, still not satisfied, persisted with her mission and asked of her new husband, "Why do your subjects not humbly bow before you as they did with my late husband, King Roderic?" Abd al-Aziz once again replied that it was not proper to do so in the Islamic religion. However, fearing he would lose her respect, he reluctantly and cleverly devised a plan. Abd al-Aziz had a small door constructed in the front of the room where he generally greeted his people. The door was built in such a manner that the people who entered the room were forced to bend or kneel in order to enter and see Abd al-Aziz. Egilona saw this as an act of deference to her husband and it seemed to quench her thirst for power and respect somewhat—while at the same time sealing the fate of Abd al-Aziz.

As fully expected, rumors began to circulate that the governor may have secretly converted to Christianity and was contemplating starting his own monarchy. Whether this was true or was fabricated by his enemies, Abd al-Aziz was ultimately beheaded by a warrior named *Ziyad ibn Udhra al-Balawi* while he was praying in the Mosque of Seville in 715–716. He was executed under the orders of Umayyad Caliph *Suleyman ibn Abd al-Malik*, who had his head sent to Damascus.

Meanwhile, *al-Ishbunah* (Lisbon) was peacefully taken by the Moors, and by 717 al-Andalus became a dependent province of the Umayyad Caliphate of Damascus. During his very brief rule, the cousin and successor to Abd al-Aziz, Governor *Ayyub ibn Habib al-*

Lakhmi, transferred the capital from Seville to Córdoba, where he set up his new residence.

In 722 the *Battle of Covadonga* took place in the northern region of Asturias between the Umayyads and Christians, where the Moors were ambushed and defeated by the legendary *Pelayo* (687–737). Pelayo was the son of a Visigoth nobleman and a relative of King Rodrigo who served as a member of the court of King Egica. Pelayo, known to the Muslims as *Belay al-Rumi* (Pelayo, the Roman), is credited as being the first key figure in what was to be the Reconquest of the Iberian Peninsula. Pelayo founded the first Christian stronghold in the Kingdom of Asturias, becoming its first king in 718 and founder of the Spanish Monarchy. In Castilian, Pelayo is usually referred to as *Don Pelayo*. "Don" is a title derived from the Latin *dominus*, meaning "lord" or "sir," as in "Don Quixote" and "Don Rodrigo." *Doña* would be its feminine form. Cádiz-born Jose Cadalso (1741–1782) described Pelayo in his work titled "Cartas Marruecas" (Moroccan Letters):

"...uno de los mejores hombres que la naturaleza ha producido."
"...one of the finest men that nature has produced."

In the year 732, another battle took place where the Moors were once again defeated. This event, known as the *Battle of Poitiers* or the *Battle of Tours*, was headed by French military leader and General *Charles Martel* (Charles the Hammer) with his Frankish troops. Poitiers, less than 200 miles from Paris, was the farthest north the Muslims ever reached. The outcome of the Battle of Poitiers served to halt the expansion of the Muslim invasion into France and more specifically into Western Europe. Ironically, today France has the highest Muslim population in Western Europe.

The Founder of al-Andalus

In the year 749/750 most of the members of the Umayyad Dynasty were massacred by the rival *Abbasid* Dynasty or *Banu Abbas* of Baghdad. This family also claimed to be descendants of the prophet Muhammad; their uncle *Abbas* founded the dynasty. Sources tell of at least 80 members of the Umayyad family, including the *Caliph Marwan II* (r. 744–750) of the Banu Ummayah from Damascus, who were led to their deaths under false pretense in the form of a dinner party held by the Abbasids, where the guests were all assassinated. One young member of the family managed to escape and, fearing for his life, immediately fled his homeland with a few members of his family. This boy was the Umayyad Prince *Abd ar-Rahman ibn Mu'awiyah ad-Dakhil*, better known as *Abd ar-Rahman I*, the grandson of *Hisham ibn Abd al-Malik*, the 10th Caliph of the Umayyad Dynasty.

Abd ar-Rahman was born in 731 in Damascus to the Umayyad prince *Mu'awiyah* and a Berber concubine named *Raha* who, like Tariq ibn Ziyad, belonged to the Nafza tribe of North Africa. The young boy was groomed at an early age, receiving a good education and a fine upbringing while earning respect and acquiring a fearless spirit that led to his exceptional leadership and conquering abilities.

Abd ar-Rahman was only 16 years of age when most of his family were slaughtered. The horrified young man fled south, surviving many ambushes and perils along the way that were implemented by the merciless Abbasids. According to *Abu Marwan ibn Hayyan*, an 11th century Hispano-Muslim historian from Córdoba, Abd ar-Rahman barely escaped with his life and a handful of members of his family: his 4-year old son *Suleyman*, a 13-year old brother named *Yahya* who was quickly captured and put to death , a sister named *Ummu al-Asbagh*, and two trusted servants and former slaves named *Bedr* and *Salim*. Abd ar-Rahman had witnessed the horror of his younger brother being tricked and beheaded by the Abbasids across the Euphrates River. Ibn Hayyan quotes Abd ar-Rahman I: "The sight of this catastrophe struck me with horror: I was seized with violent fears for my life, and began to run with all my speed; my feet scarcely touched the ground; I flew rather than ran."

The prince continued his hazardous journey, finding refuge with Bedouin desert tribes as he headed towards Morocco, the land of his mother, where he hoped to find sympathy and support as an Umayyad.

Straits of Gibraltar

After five years in exile and countless narrow escapes from spies and traps set by the Abbasids, vvAtbd ar-Rahman I finally crossed the Straits of Gibraltar from Ceuta and disembarked in 755 at *al-Munakkab* (Almuñécar, Granada).

Well received he was, as there were many Syrian settlers and supporters of the Umayyads already livaing here, particularly in *Elvira* or *Gharnatah* (Granada), to welcome the sole Umayyad heir. During his treacherous journey from Damascus to Almuñécar, the prince had greatly matured as a man and strengthened as a warrior.

The Jewish astrologer who advised *Ibn Habib al-Fehri*, governor of North Africa between 745 and 755, predicted that "a young family member of the Marwan, descended from kings, shall in time become a great conqueror; he shall found in Andalus an empire for him and his posterity; his name is Abd ar-Rahman, and he wears two long curls." He was correct, as in the year 756 Abd ar-Rahman proclaimed himself Emir and declared al-Andalus a state independent from the Caliphate of Damascus; and he became the founder of the Spanish Umayyad Dynasty. Al-Andalus was taking on its own singular identity as ties with the Caliphate were weakening. The new emir set up his court in Córdoba, establishing a successful dynasty that was to last nearly three centuries.

Almuñécar

Muslim Andalusi historian *Ibn Idhari* of the late 13th century wrote the classic *Historia de los Reyes de al-Andalus y de Marruecos* (History of the Kings of al-Andalus and Morocco), where he described the physical attributes of several Umayyad rulers of al-Andalus. Abd ar-Rahman grew to be tall and slim and always dressed in white with a turban of the same color. It has been written that the half-Syrian and half-Berber prince had a characteristic mole on his face and a poor sense of smell; and like Tariq ibn Ziyad, was blind in one eye. Abd ar-Rahman had reddish-blond hair that was inherited from his mother which he wore in the form of two ringlets. Regarding his nature, he was said to be most eloquent, perceptive, generous, merciful, and kind-hearted. He had refined tastes and was a patron of the arts and sciences. Abd ar-Rahman was skilled in poetry as well as in the military arts. It is said that he took the time to visit the sick, attend funerals, recite prayers, and pray with his people. His wife was named *Khazraf* and/or *Zaibra*, however, very little is known about either.

In Almuñécar today stands an imposing bronze statue of the founder of al-Andalus, *Abderahman I*, as he is known in Castilian. The commanding statue is situated at the base of the large rock formation known as *El Peñón del Santo* (Cliff of the Saint) where breathtaking views of the Mediterranean Sea can be appreciated. Prior to 2005, the statue bore the following inscription:

> *El 15 de agosto de 755 DC, Abderrahman I 'El Emigrante' procedente de Damasco por la Playa de Almuñécar, siendo el creador del floreciente Estado de al-Andalus.*

> On the 15 of August of 755 ADE, Abd ar-Rahman I 'The Emigrant' originating from Damascus through the Beach of Almuñécar, became the creator of the flourishing state of al-Andalus.

Abd ar-Rahman I

After the 1250th anniversary of his arrival, in 2005, his statue in Almuñécar has been given two new plaques inscribed in both Spanish and English. I have left the translation exactly as it reads:

Abd ar-Rahman I

Único superviviente de los Omeya, tras la mantaza de su familia. Arribo a las costas de Almuñécar el 15 de Agosto de 755.

Proclamo el Emirato de Córdoba, independiente de Bagdad, iniciando una dinastía en al-Andalus que alcanzaría momentos de gran esplendor.

El Ayuntamiento de Almuñécar erigió esta estatua a su figure, obra del escultor granadino Miguel Moreno.

Almuñécar, Octubre 2005

En el MCCL Aniversario de su llegada a nuestras playas

Abd ar-Rahman I

The only survivor of the Umayyad dynasty, he landed on the coast of Almuñécar on the 15th August, 755.

Later he founded the Emirate of Córdoba, which was independent of Bagdad and so beginning a new dynasty in al-Andalus which achieved moments of great splendor.

Almuñécar town hall erected this statue in his honour. This statue is a piece of work by Miguel Moreno a sculptor from Granada.

Almuñécar, October 2005

On the 1250th anniversary of his arrival to our shores

Abd ar-Rahman built a spectacular palatial residence in Córdoba that he named *ar-Rusafah*, after his royal residence in Damascus of the same name which he greatly missed. His statue in Almuñécar bears his quote:

Oh Palmera!
Tu eres como yo
Extranjera en occidente
Alejada de tu patria.
    Abderahman I

Oh Palm Tree!
Like me, you are
A stranger in the west
Far away from your homeland.

Abd ar-Rahman I

Abd ar-Rahman

Few samples of his poetry have survived and in this short verse, his powerful feelings of nostalgia are exposed as he addresses a magnificent date palm tree that he planted in the spectacular gardens of his palace of ar-Rusafah in Córdoba. The exact location of this palace is unknown; however, recent geophysical surveys in the area just south of the National Parador of Córdoba have revealed the possible ruins of a large building that could have been the royal residence of the founder of al-Andalus.

According to Ibn Hayyan, "he [also] supplied his capital with water, built himself a palace, and erected mosques, baths, bridges, and castles in every province of his dominions." Abd ar-Rahman I died on September 30, in 788, leaving twenty children behind. He is said to have been buried at the main Mosque of Córdoba that he greatly expanded but did not live to see completed. He is known in history as the "Falcon of Andalus" and received the moniker of *ad-Dakhil* or "the Emigrant."

Abd ar-Rahman I was succeeded by his favorite son *Hisham I* rather than his eldest son, Suleyman. Hisham I was born from a concubine and freed slave of Visigoth ancestry named *Halal* who converted to Islam. Upon the death of Hisham in 796, another son, *al-Hakam I*, inherited the title until his death in 822. We known that a remarkable concubine of his, named *Ayab*, constructed a small mosque and founded a hospital for lepers in Córdoba.

Next in line to assume the title of Emir was *Abd ar Rahman II*, son of al-Hakam I and a woman named *Halaweh* ("Sweet"). Abd ar-Rahman II was born in *Tulaytulah* (Toledo) and was considered a generous and liberal man who was quite fond of poetry and music. He grew to be a cultured man, a dynamic warrior, and an exceptional ruler.

> Abd ar-Rahman II was a tall, attractive, and corpulent man with reddish blond hair and big dark blue eyes. It is documented that he wore a long beard that he dyed dark red with al-heña (henna). He married at least two of his concubines, Mudathirah and Ashifa. Ashifa, who bore him a son, is documented as being his favorite. Abd ar-Rahman II also married a woman named Kahtaz who would be the mother of his successor. It has been estimated that Abd ar-Rahman II had over 50 concubines in his harem and 87 children. Some of these women included the Faur, Muammara, and the "three Madinites." This last group of three

(Alam, Qalam, and the favorite Fadl), were not only beautiful women but highly educated, talented musicians, singers, and a poetess as well being inseparable from the Emir. These women accompanied Abd ar-Rahman II on his outings, a privilege previously held exclusively by the mother of his heir. However, Abd ar-Rahman II had yet another favorite concubine named *Tarub*. His passion for her not only cost him dearly but may have cost him his life.

The Sultana Tarub was of remarkable beauty and exerted a great amount of influence over the smitten Abd ar-Rahman II, who sought her approval in all matters pertaining to the harem. He named her "Tarub," which translates as "enchanted" or "bewitched," as he so strongly felt about her.

The Emir often bestowed impressive gifts on the women of his harem. To Tarub, he gave a magnificent pearl necklace that he purchased for 10,000 gold dinares. This piece of jewellery had once belonged to *Zobeida*, the wife of the Abbasid Caliph *Harun ar-Rashid* (the ruler depicted in the stories of *One Thousand and One Nights* or *Arabian Nights*). Abd ar-Rahman II spent many nights with Tarub and she bore him a son, whom they named *Abd-Allah*, who was apparently weak in nature and corrupt in morals.

Muslim chronicles tell the story of how Tarub came to be quite angry at the Emir on one occasion and locked herself in her pavilion for days, refusing to open the door to him. In desperation, Abd ar-Rahman II decided to persuade her with bags full of thousands of silver dirhams that he had stacked high up against her door. When Tarub finally decided to open the door, countless bags of coins toppled over each other, spilling tens of thousands of dirhams all around her. She, with great joy, immediately fell to her knees, kissed the feet of Abd ar-Rahman II, and all was forgiven.

At the time of the Emir's death, there was a considerable amount of intrigue involving Tarub and a cruel eunuch named *Abu l-Fath Nasr*. Eunuchs were generally employed within the harems and were often close confidants of the women. Chronicles tell of Nasr and Tarub conspiring together in an unsuccessful plot to place her son Abd Allah upon the throne two years before Abd ar-Rahman II became Emir. The mistress and the eunuch intended to poison the

Emir; however, the plot was exposed by *Fajr*, a beautiful woman in his harem. Nasr died by the very poison he was planning to use against Abd ar-Rahman II, in his presence.

Nevertheless, around 850 the health of Abd ar-Rahman II was faltering and on his deathbed, he named one of his sons as successor. The Emir died in Córdoba in 852, and immediately the principal eunuchs gathered; swearing on the Koran, they fulfilled the wishes of Abd ar-Rahman II, passing on the title of Emir to his son, Prince Muhammad. That very night, Muhammad arrived at the Alcázar and was proclaimed the new Emir.

The Founder of Mayrit

By the late 8th century, the territory of al-Andalus covered the entire Iberian Peninsula save for the northern Basque regions, Asturias and part of Catalonia. A highly regarded Muslim Andalusí named *Ahmad ibn Muhammad ar-Razi* (887–995), known as "El Moro Rasis" (Rasis the Moor), authored a geographical description of al-Andalus where he states: "In its territory there are numerous castles and cities, such as the castle of Mayrit." This quote and others were recompiled by ibn Hayyan in his third volume of a series of ten titled *al-Kitab al-Muqtabis fi-Ta'rikh al-Andalus* (The Book of the Scholar on the History of al-Andalus): "Muhammad (I) was, for the people of the frontier of Toledo, who constructed the castle of Talamanca, and the castle of Mayrit and Peñafora." Ibn Hayyan, whose father was a secretary to General *Al-Mansur*, is considered as one of the most important historians of al-Andalus. His work is believed to be the first reference to the history of al-Andalus that was consulted by medieval Christian historians.

Originally Madrid was believed to have been founded by the Greeks and Romans. The fact that Madrid was founded by the Moors was not confirmed until as late in history as 1944 when a previously unknown text written by a 14th century Muslim geographer and historian named *Ibn Abd al-Mun'im al-Himyari* was brought to light. His work, titled *Kitab ar-Rawd al-Mi'tar* (*The Book of the Fragrant Garden*) became an invaluable source of information regarding Islamic Spain, although the idea that Madrid was founded by the

Moors had appeared at least twice in other publications during the early 1900s without raising much attention.

Al-Himyari based his research on other historians including ibn Hayyan and 12ᵗʰ century geographer *Abu Abd Allah Muhammad al-Idrisi*. Al-Himyari affirms: "Mayrit, constructed by the Emir of Córdoba, Muhammad I, was a small town containing an impenetrable fortress and a major mosque." He further states: "Mayrit, notable city of al-Andalus, had the strongest and best defensive architecture that existed at this time."

Additional confirmation appears in the "Anonymous Description of al-Andalus" that was written between 1344 and 1487. "In the outskirts of Toledo lies the city (Medina) of Madrid, of average importance, but very well fortified, founded by Muhammad I b. Abd al- [*sic*] Rahman al-Awsat."

Muhammad I or *Muhammad ibn Abd ar-Rahman al-Awsat* was born in Córdoba during the year 822/3 He was the great grandson of the founder of al-Andalus, and the son of Abd ar-Rahman II and his wife Kahtaz. Muhammad I became the 5ᵗʰ independent Emir of Córdoba.

According to ibn Hayyan, Muhammad I was a skilled and avid chess player who often played with a servant named *Aidun*. He was also an educated man, fond of mathematics, sciences, arts, poetry, and literature. It was overheard that the favorite Vizier of the Emir, *Hasim ibn Abd al-'Aziz*, once said to him: "Son of all Caliphs, what a pleasant life it would be if not for death!" To which the Emir replied, "Son of the infidel! Incorrect are your words! Would we possess this power that we have if it were not for death?" Muhammad I continued, "If it were not for death, we would never rule!"

The Emir was of a fair and rosy complexion, a short man with a small head and a full beard. Muhammad I is further described as being generous, kind, patient, modest, and virtuous; however, he displayed very little tolerance towards those who went against Islam as his obsession with preserving the Emirate in al-Andalus paralleled his profound love of the sciences and arts. Muhammad I was considered far less liberal than his father had been and was described by some as somewhat cruel and narrow-minded.

"Muhammad I" by José Flores

When the Moors arrived in the area of Madrid, they discovered an archaic village of hunters and shepherds and promptly converted the site into an important military and agricultural settlement. The Alcázar stood on a hill on the left bank of the Manzanares River. It followed the typical scheme of Muslim fortresses, being situated in a prominent position where approaching enemies could easily be detected. The fortress of *Mayrit* was raised on a hillside that enabled the surveillance of the road that traveled between the region of Toledo and the Guadarrama Mountains. Researcher, scholar, historian, and author J. Oliver Asín (1905–1980), an expert and leading authority in the study of Moorish Madrid, states that the fortress of Mayrit and Talamankah were actually built to protect the main road that connected Toledo with Medinaceli (Soria) via the Jarama Valley through constant vigilance over the territory between Madrid and the Guadarrama Sierra on the route to Medinaceli.

Around the year 865, the Emir fulfilled his duties successfully and ordered the construction of a small but impregnable fortress and citadel surrounded by a sturdy protective wall in what would be named Mayrit. During the late 9th century, the central frontier territory of the *Marca Media* or Middle March (*al-Tagr al-Awsat*) of al-Andalus was composed of three main settlements: Mayrit (of the Manzanares Valley), Talamankah (of the Jarama Valley), and *Qal'at Abd es-Salam* (Alcalá de Henares, formerly the Roman Complutum, of the Henares Valley). A "marca" or "march" was a defensive region established by the Caliphate of Córdoba that separated Muslim Spain or al-Andalus from the smaller Christian kingdoms. Mérida was the capital of the *Marca Inferior* or Lower March (*al-Tagr al-Gharbi*) and *Sarakusta* (Zaragoza) became the capital of the *Marca Superior* or Upper March (*al-Tagr al-A'la*.) These three marches or tactical zones of al-Andalus were united by the main road that connected Mérida with Zaragoza that passed through Toledo. Mayrit, Talamankah, and Qal'at Abd es-Salam were all situated on the three main roadways of the Middle March that were under the jurisdiction of Toledo, the capital of the Middle March during the 9th and 10th centuries.

Other fortresses or *hisns* along with Mayrit that arose within the territory during the 8th and 9th century raised by Abd ar-Rahman II and Muhammad I included *Qal'at Jalifah* (Catalifa), *Qal'at Rabah* (Calatrava la Vieja), *Talavaira* (Talavera de la Reina), *Salmantica* (Salamanca), *Peñafora, Esteras de Medinaceli* (Soria), *Qal'at al-Ayyub* (Calatayud), and *Zorita de los Canes*.

The small Christian and Jewish population of al-Andalus was known as *dhimmies* or "protected ones." Although the dhimmies were able to maintain their religious beliefs and practices, they were subjected to numerous restrictions such as paying a special census tax known as *jizyah* that was collected by their Muslim rulers. The jizyah was a personal tax based upon the individual's means or worth. Another territorial tax, known as *kharaj*, was charged for any agricultural property or land owned. Regardless of one's faith, the death penalty was given to anyone who spoke ill of Islam or the prophet Muhammad. It is interesting to note that Muhammad I did not impose further rules restricting the Jewish population, as he had done with the Christians, as he believed that the Jews posed no threat to Islam.

During the reign of his father Abd ar-Rahman II, Muhammad I participated in several military expeditions that prepared him for battles and leadership. When Abd ar-Rahman II conquered Zaragoza in 844, he appointed his son Muhammad governor. His military experience was soon to be tested, as just nine months into his generally peaceful reign several episodes of internal turmoil arose. There were uprisings in Toledo. The Emir had inherited from his father a number of rebellious separatist movements from the *Mozárabes* and *Muladíes*.

The Mozárabes, fighting for the kingdom they had lost at the Battle of Guadalete, were descendants of Visigoth Christians and Hispano-Romans who maintained their Catholic faith during Islamic rule and formed an alliance with the Asturians. The Muladíes were descendants of Spanish Visigoths who had reluctantly accepted Islam; they were known as "converts" and they were fervent in making their land independent of Córdoba throughout the rule of Muhammad I. Muladí families such as the powerful *Banu Qasi*, a Basque-Muslim tribe descended from the Visigoths that prospered in the upper Ebro Valley, were involved in frequent conflicts with the Umayyads during the 9th and 10th centuries, particularly with the governor of Tudela, *Musa ibn Musa Qasi*. Musa, appointed governor of Zaragoza by Muhammad I, was removed from his position by the Emir in 860 and died two years later.

Upon the death of his father Abd ar-Rahman II in 852, the Toledans seized the opportunity and began another revolt. The moment Muhammad I became Emir, he began imposing upon the Christians laws and restrictions that had never before been enforced in al-Andalus or that were no longer implemented. Yet between the years 850 and 859, a small group of Christians from Córdoba in the form of priests and monks publicly denounced Islam and maligned the prophet Muhammad. The Emir retaliated by ordering all new churches to be destroyed and sentencing 48 Orthodox Christians to death by decapitation or fire for going against Islam. This group of clergymen became known as the *Martyrs of Córdoba*.

In 854, the Toledans, who had joined forces with Asturian King Ordoño I, went as far as to imprison their governor and partly destroy the fortress of Calatrava. Muhammad I with his soldiers retaliated and in June of 854 the Toledans and Asturians were ultimately defeated at what became known as the *Battle of Guadacelete*. It has been written that the Emir "slew twenty thousand Toledans and twenty thousand infidels." This event that took place southeast of Toledo is known in history as the *Day of Guadalete*. Four years later and to the great disappointment of the citizens of Toledo, the Emir destroyed the Alcántara Bridge over the Tagus River, causing many deaths.

Another revolt during his rule led the Emir to consider executing all Christian men and selling their women into slavery unless they converted to Islam. His advisors, however, advised him to abandon the extreme idea. Regardless, he went ahead and replaced Christian officials who did not convert to Islam with Muslim officials; the Christians lost their prestigious positions within the administration.

It is only fair to mention at this point that while the Moors created the flourishing and prosperous land of al-Andalus, much blood was spilt by their hands. Muslim troops were often merciless, decapitating their enemies whether they were injured, imprisoned, or dead, and displayed their heads to the public in major cities of al-Andalus as both trophies and warnings. Amongst themselves, Al-Mansur and Emir Abd-Allah executed at least one of their sons, as did Caliph Abd ar-Rahman III, who also executed 300 of his army officials by decapitation and nailing their heads to crosses after the .Battle of Simancas in 939 for not being sufficiently heroic.

Muhammad I dispatched several military expeditions throughout the Iberian Peninsula against those who opposed Islam and the Umayyad Emirate. He participated in several military campaigns in such towns as *Banbilunah* (Pamplona), *Meridah* (Merida), *Batalyaws* (Badajoz), *Jalikiyyah* (Galicia), *Liyun* (León), *Barshelonah* (Barcelona), and *Sarakusta* (Zaragoza.) The Emir's punishments included increasing taxes, confiscating properties, and sentencing many people to death.

Serious threats to the Umayyads were also posed by another Muladí, the rebellious leader named *Umar ibn Hafsun*; his revolt began in the year 880. Hafsun, from the mountains of *ar-Runda* (Ronda) in Málaga, was well known as a local bandit. Many bandits or *bandoleros* operated in the area between the 16th and 20th centuries; the only museum in the country today dedicated to bandits, the *Museo Del Bandolero*, is situated in Ronda.

Ronda Bridge

After this battle the Emir constructed, within the strategic central area of the peninsula, the customary and traditional Islamic *Alcázar* (castle) and *Alcazába* (military zone or compound). It is estimated that Mayrit was built between 860 and 871, as by this date it already had a governor. Several authors give 865 as the most probable year that Mayrit was founded.

The Muslims erected a series of fortified watchtowers or *atalayas* between the 9th and 10th centuries and established strategic look-out points at various locations. The defensive site of Mayrit was part of a chain or network of fortified positions and watchtowers positioned around the center of the peninsula at approximately every 25 miles. These cylindrical towers had two or more interior levels with an indoor staircase that was situated upon an elevated level. Two soldiers were assigned to each watchtower to guard the Guadarrama Valley against any approaching rebellious Toledans from the south and Christians from the north.

The Muslims used the same network of roads as the Visigoths, the roads that were originally constructed by the Romans. The area became fortified during the last quarter of the 9th century and became a *ribat* or a religious and military community and frontier town of al-Andalus. Mayrit did not become a *medina* or city until nearly a century after the wall was built during the prosperous rule of Abd ar-Rahman III.

According to historians, the Alcázar of Mayrit was rectangular in shape with two courtyards or patios and four semi-circular towers on the western side, two square towers in the southern side, and another square tower on the northwest corner. Mayrit was well defended with its protective walls, solid gates, sturdy watchtowers, and various lookout points. From here, the Muslim soldiers were able to keep a watch over nearly the entire Manzanares region and were therefore able to be well prepared for attacks from Christian troops as they entered through the Sierra del Guadarrama. By smoke signals during the day and bonfires at night, the various garrisons communicated with each other and warned of possible impending attacks. When Christian troops advanced, the citizens of surrounding areas found refuge behind the city walls.

Although the Battle of Guadalete was a victory for Muhammad I, he did not attempt to conquer Toledo, nor was he able to force the Toledans into total submission. He had, however, proved that he was able to carry on his father's military and religious campaigns despite the rebellions from the Christians in the north, the Mozárabes, and the Muladíes, that persisted throughout his entire reign.

Muhammad I not only founded what was to be the capital of the country centuries later but continued to fight the battles his father had fought while carrying on and completing his father's extensive building projects that included the expansion of the great Mosque in Córdoba. Muhammad I died in Córdoba on August 4, 886, after a 35-year reign; he was laid to rest in the gardens of the Alcázar of Córdoba with his ancestors.

Alcázar Gardens Córdoba

Muhammad I not only selected the site of Mayrit for its strategic location but the area itself possessed an abundance of water that flowed from the numerous surrounding springs, streams, and wells that existed since pre-history. The central region of the Iberian Peninsula was an extensive area of low hills and meadowlands with plentiful streams and rivers that were highly conducive to lush vegetation. The Muslims encountered a land abandoned by the Visigoths who primarily excelled at hunting, but the Moors knew how to take advantage of the richness of the land. It was not long before Mayrit became known for its green landscape, abundant gardens, flourishing orchards, and highly efficient agricultural techniques.

Those who were not involved in the military field turned to farming and agriculture for income while others engaged in business transactions involving handicrafts, pottery, and commodities. However, farming and agriculture became the fundamental drivers of the economy and excellent hunting, crop-growing, and cattle-raising conditions eventually added an agricultural element to the existing military character of Mayrit.

However, the Alcázar of Mayrit needed water and the Manzanares River was at the bottom of the hill where the Alcázar stood. Muhammad I corrected the situation by building subterranean channels for irrigation purposes. These complex networks of underground canals brought water to the population and surrounding areas from springs and wells miles away, perfecting a system of channels connected to a series of suctioning wells that extracted water through gravity, a method that was created first by the Persians.

Muhammad I ordered the construction of such an underground water channel in Mayrit to supply water to the town. This device known as a *Qanat* or *Mayra* was introduced into al-Andalus by way of Mayrit; and here lie the origins of the name of the Madrid that will be later explored. In general, a Qanat measured about three feet in width and roughly six feet in height, with a depth of 180 feet.. These wells collected water and were connected by underground chambers that were generally constructed from brick.

Although Mayrit was well known for its Qanats, they did exist elsewhere in the peninsula such as in Granada and Valencia; however, none were as extensive or sophisticated as the originals that were constructed in Mayrit during the rule of Muhammad I.

Many such underground water channels were dug after the 12th century. One in particular that was discovered at Plaza de los Carros (Plaza of the Wagons) in old Madrid is dated to the 10th century or possibly earlier, during the rule of Muhammad I. This Mayra measuring about 32 feet in length was unearthed in 1983 and forms part of the most important findings of Islamic Madrid as it is the first of its kind documented within the Iberian Peninsula. Two other significant Qanats in Madrid that were discovered are *Los Caños Viejos*, by the church of San Pedro, belonging to the Christian Era, and *Los Caños del Peral*, that is likely from the Moorish Era.

The Almudena

During the second half of the 9th century, Mayrit functioned as a small yet outstanding fortress or fortified urban center. South of the Alcázar, where the *Qadi* or governor resided, was the *Almudena* (al-Mudayna), as it was named after the Christian conquest. This first precinct, or *Alcazába* as it is also called, measured around 4 hectares (although other sources have this figure as 9 hectares). Within you would find the Alcázar, the residence of the governor, and the mosque.

Virgen de la Almudena Cathedral

The small neighborhood of the Almudena was composed of twisting lanes with tightly packed houses that were situated within the walled area below and including the Alcázar and major mosque. Here a small military population lived that has been estimated at approximately 2500 inhabitants. A population comprised of guards and soldiers along with their families settled in the area where the royal palace and the Almudena Cathedral stand today. Once the defensive wall was constructed, the status of Mayrit as a defensive outpost or "hisn" was elevated to that of an Almudena. It was at this point in the history of Madrid that the fortified village of Mayrit was born.

The first defensive wall of Madrid, built under the orders of Muhammad I, is known as *La Muralla de Madrid* or "the Wall of Madrid." The original structure was about 12 feet thick built with irregular blocks of flint rock that were cemented with a solid and strong mixture of lime, water, and sand. Ibn Hayyan relates that when construction of the wall began, remains of a giant prehistoric elephant were found inside a massive pit outside the wall, to the great astonishment the local population.

The protective wall extended from the Alcázar south to Cuesta de la Vega, and Cuesta de Ramón to the streets of Pretil de los Consejos, del Factor (or de la Almudena by other accounts), altos de Rebeque, to Bailén and back to the starting point of the Alcázar, although there are slightly different versions according to various sources.

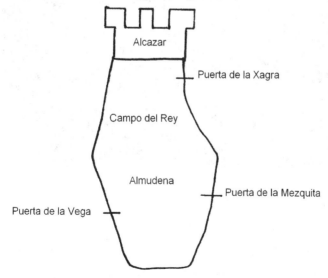

Almudena Cathedral behind Moorish Wall

The Castilian word for "street" is *calle* (pronounced KA-yeh) and is written in the abbreviated form of "c/" followed by the name of the street; for example Segovia Street is written as *c/ Segovia*. From here on, the streets of Madrid will be written in this manner.

Access to Mayrit was through three main gates within the wall that connected the area to the outside world. To the southwest was *Puerta de la Vega*, to the southeast was *Puerta de la Mezquita*, and to the northeast was the less frequently used *Puerta de la Xagra* situated closest to the Alcázar.

Puerta de la Vega or *Alvega* faced the fertile plain known as a "vega" in Castilian. This gate was approximately situated on the curve formed by Cuesta de la Vega and c/ Mayor (that was then a street dedicated to commerce named *Guadalajara*). Puerta de la Vega is the earliest documented gate of the Muslim wall that was referred to as *portam albegam* in 1152. This gate stood at the very spot that is occupied today by the crypt of the Almudena Cathedral. Puerta de la Vega survived the longest of the three gates as it was the most durable covered with sturdy sheets of iron. It is believed that it was through this gate that Alfonso VI entered and conquered Mayrit. Puerta de la Vega was expanded and reconstructed several times, until it was permanently demolished around 1814.

Historian and writer Jerónimo de Quintana (1570–1644) and native of Madrid described it as follows:

> *La Puerta de la Vega duro hasta nuestro tiempos; miraba al Occidente, que por descubrirse desde ella una gran vega a la parte del rió, tomo de ella el nombre. Era angosta y estaba debajo de una fuerte torre caballera; tenía dos estancias, y en el hueco de la de adentro había dos escaleras a los dos lados, en cada uno la suya muy angostas, por donde se subía a lo alto. En la de fuera había en el punto del arco, un agujero, donde tenían de secreto una gran pesa de hierro, que en tiempo de guerra, con algún trabuco o torno dejaban caer con violencia, dejando a los que hallaban debajo mil menuzos. En medio de las dos estancias estaban las puertas, guarnecidas con una recia hoja de hierro, una muy fuerte de clavazón.*

The Gate of the Vega survived until our times; it looked out to the west and it was visible from a big fertile plain by the river, from which it took its name. It was narrow and underneath was a strong and noble tower; it had two rooms, and in the space inside of one were two staircases at each side, each very narrow, where one would climb to the top. In the outer one, there was a hole in the arch where they secretly kept a large weight made of steel, that in times of war, with a clamp or lathe, could be dropped with great violence, smashing those who were below into 1000 pieces. In the center of the two rooms were the gates, embellished with a thick sheet of steel, a very strong one of them made of nails.

Puerta de la Mezquita or Gate of the Mosque was situated where c/ Mayor and c/ del Sacramento meet, facing c/ del Factor, as it was here where the principal Mosque was situated. Al-Idrisi tells us, "At the foot of the hill lies Madrid, small city and fortress well defended and prosperous, that in the Muslim era contained a mosque where orations were regularly given."

After the Christian conquest, the gate was renamed *Arco de la Almudena* or *Arco de Santa Maria* because of its proximity to the church of Santa Maria. This gate was demolished during the 16th century, when King Felipe II ordered it to be taken down to widen the path for the grand entrance of his wife Queen Ana of Austria. Its stones were actually used in the reconstruction of the Alcázar.

Puerta de la Xagra or *Asagra* was located in the zone of La Plaza de Oriente by the gardens of the royal palace on c/ Bailén. This gate faced the farmland or *xagra* that was less populated to the north and provided access to the military zone and Alcázar. Puerta de la Xagra, situated close to where the Jewish population lived, was first mentioned in documents dated to 1190 as *portam de sacra*. The gate was demolished during the mid 16th century and on c/ *de Rebeque*, you will find this sign:

Across the Alcázar was the vacant area that served as a training camp for the troops, where Plaza de la Armería is situated today; and to the south was the *Almagil* or mosque. Within the area were all the necessities such as grain houses, tanneries, and blacksmiths shops for the manufacturing of weapons. Due to the growing needs and demands of the early military population, Mayrit further attracted a small community of farmers, merchants, blacksmiths, and carpenters that would cater to such needs. Among the citizens, you would also find weavers, bakers, barbers, jewelers, shoemakers, tailors, artisans, and pottery-makers. Within Mayrit, the Mozárabe population settled by the Church of San Andrés.

Puerta de la Xagra

The Moors introduced the methods of pottery glazing, enamel coating, and the highly decorative technique known as "dry cord" to the Peninsula. It was not long before Mayrit also became known for producing the finest ceramics in al-Andalus. Fifteenth-century Arab geographer Al-Himyari wrote about the remarkable clay of Mayrit:

> *Hay en Mayrit una tierra de la que se hacen pucheros, los cuales se pueden utilizar, poniéndolos al fuego, durante veinte años, sin que se rompan. El alimento que en ellos se deposita no se altera además con el calor de la atmósfera.*

> There is in Mayrit a type of earth that pots are made of, that can be used when placing them upon fire for 20 years without breaking. The food that is deposited therein does not become altered even with the heat of the atmosphere.

Earthenware and other household items have been discovered in silos that were used for underground storage in the areas of Cuesta de la Vega, c/ del Espejo, c/ Cava Baja, c/ del Almendro, c/

de Segovia, and Plaza de los Carros, to name a few. Objects found included glazed pots, jars, vats, pitchers, cups, large bowls, plates, and oil lamps.

4. Mayrit, 10ᵀᴴ –11ᵀᴴ Centuries

Emir Muhammad I was succeeded by his son, *Al-Mundhir*, whose mother was a dark-skinned concubine named *Athl*. Al-Mundhir ruled for two years until he was murdered by his brother *Abd Allah*, who succeeded him. Abd Allah was the Emir's son by his wife *Ishar*. Ishar lived to be 93 years old, dying a year before her son Abd Allah in 911. Abd Allah selected his favored grandson, Abd ar-Rahman III (r. 912–961), to be his successor.

Abd ar-Rahman III was 21 years old when he inherited the title of Emir and in the year 929, he proclaimed himself the first Caliph of Islamic Spain. Abd ar-Rahman III had a very light complexion with dark blue eyes; his self-consciousness was evident as he dyed his red hair black to appear Moorish. The Caliph had a cruel streak which he often displayed to prisoners, the women of his harem, and to one of his sons—whom he had executed. Muslim chronicles however, describe him as being prudent, amiable, highly respected, of good taste, just, generous, and gentle. Abd ar-Rahman III is known in history as a remarkable ruler who converted the Umayyad capital of Córdoba into the most influential intellectual center in Western Europe. He is regarded as the greatest of all the Mohammedan rulers of Spain.

The Caliph was quite fond of literature, arts, and architecture, and around 936, he built the palatial city of *Medina az-Zahara*, just over three miles west from old Córdoba. This magnificent complex, named after his favorite concubine Zahra, was modeled after the royal palace in Damascus. Another of his favorite concubines, named *Muryan*, who became the mother of his successor al-Hakam II, was quite a woman as she had two small mosques built in Córdoba.

Medina az-Zahara

Three years into the reign of Abd ar-Rahman III, the walls of the Alcázar of Mayrit were destroyed by the Christian troops of King Ramiro II of León (r. 931–951.) In 932, Ramiro II temporarily occupied the area outside the wall but was unable to infiltrate the fortress. He is regarded as the first Christian to attack Mayrit and in the "Crónica del Monje de Silos" (Chronicles of the Monk of Silos) dated c. 1110 ADE, Ramiro II is described as "...marching to the city they called Mayrit with his troops, dismantling its walls, creating much destruction and returning to his kingdom at peace with his victory."

Eight years later Mayrit was rebuilt and reinforced by Abd ar-Rahman III when the Moors recaptured the Alcázar after the Christian victory at the *Battle of Simancas* in the summer of 939. In 950, just before his death, Ramiro II launched another unsuccessful expedition against Mayrit with the help of Count Fernán González of Castile who earlier, in 924, had attempted to attack Mayrit but was unable to complete the mission, let alone enter Muslim Madrid.

The *ribat* or small fortification of Mayrit was quick to acquire status within the Muslim territory as it assumed its role as the frontier town of the central zone in the Middle March of al-Andalus with its capital in Toledo. This territory roughly included Ciudad Real, Guadalajara, Soria, and Segovia as well.

Continuous battles took place within the Middle March between the Moors and Muladíes and by the end of the 10th century the population of al-Andalus was mostly comprised of Muladíes. Mayrit existed as a Muslim fortification for a little over two centuries as a modest walled city or Almudena. As the town began to significantly expand during the second half of the 10th century and early 11th century, suburbs or *arrabales* outside the walled city emerged as a result.

The Arrabales

The population of these suburbs or arrabales was steadily rising due to the expanding mixture of the civil and military population. Eventually the arrival of scientists, intellects, and scholars who chose Mayrit as a central point of their activity further put Mayrit on the map, resulting in the expansion and increase in the number of nearby suburbs. Just prior to the Christian conquest, it has been estimated that the population reached just over 12,400 inhabitants. The inhabitants of Mayrit, as throughout al-Andalus, consisted of Arabs at the top of the social scale followed by, in descending order, Berbers, Muladíes, Mozárabes, and Jews.

Archaeological excavations have determined that there may have been at least four arrabales in Madrid between the 9th and 12th centuries. Before the conquest of Mayrit during the 11th century, the first and largest arrabal was home to the Christian Mozárabes. This population was mainly comprised of merchants, administrators, financial officers, and craftsmen. The Mozárabes settled in the area located south by the hill of Las Vistillas below the viaduct, where they founded the church of San Andrés, as the Muslims tolerated their worshipping according to the Catholic religion. The arrabal was well populated as it permitted easy access to the city through the Puerta de la Vega. This is the region that was to be inhabited by the Muslims during Christian rule that, from the 15th century onward, was known as the *Morería Vieja* (old Muslim quarter).

It was during the 10th and 11th centuries that a new style of architecture arose from the lack of churches throughout the newly created Christian Spain. This style is known as *Romanesque* and fine examples can be found in Zamora, Salamanca, Aragón, Ávila, Burgos, Segovia, Huesca, Asturias, Galicia, and Santiago de Compostela.

During the 11th century, suburbs began to emerge outside the walled enclosure, as numerous ceramics discovered in these areas have proven. Further archeological remains have been found in various silos that served as long-term storage for grain and domestic items; they were also used to store refuse between the 9th and 11th centuries. These silos contained broken and whole ceramics that were unearthed in several surrounding streets and plazas.

By the 11th or early 12th century, the Christians extended and enlarged the city wall, expanding the Almudena until it measured approximately 35 hectares. At this time, the arrabales of the old medina were now included within the second walled precinct. These new suburbs or arrabales arose by the communities belonging to the local parishes and therefore received their names, such as the arrabales and churches that later arose of San Ginés, San Andrés, Santa Cruz, and San Martín. Another suburb within the walled area that is mentioned in 1190 is the arrabal of San Miguel, near the Puerta de la Xagra of the Muslim wall. By the second half of the 11th century, the small military village of Mayrit was completely transformed into an urban nucleus.

There is evidence that several arrabales existed near the Almudena that extended around the Puerta de la Mezquita. Towards the east, the small arrabal known as *Axarquía*, mentioned in 10th century documents, was situated outside the walled area by Puerta de la Xagra. During the 16th century this suburb was the location of a meat market. The name of "Axarquía" is derived from the Arabic *as-sharqiyya* that translates to "the east," just as the name of "Algarve" in Portugal is derived from *al-Gharb*, "the west," for its location within the peninsula.

In Muslim Madrid as throughout al-Andalus, the *hammam* or public bath houses served as a social place for relaxation and conversation as well as for ablutions as part of the daily religious and purifying rituals. The capital city of Córdoba alone is estimated to have had 800 bath houses during the 10th century. One bathing establishment in Mayrit was located on *Caños Viejos* near the Church of San Pedro and c/ Segovia that existed during the 12th century or possibly earlier.

Hygiene is regarded by the Muslims as an expression of faith and devotion as they believe that cleanliness purifies both body and soul. It was often said that a Moor would gladly sacrifice his food for a bar of soap. What must the Muslims have thought when Queen Isabella I decided in 1491 to wear the exact same dress every day until Granada, the last Muslim stronghold in the Iberian Peninsula, was conquered in 1492? Or that she herself claimed to have bathed twice in her lifetime, the day of her birth and the day of her marriage?

Within the bath houses, it was strictly prohibited for the men to mix with the women. The men would visit during the morning and in the afternoons it was reserved for the women and their young children. Here, the women tended to their hygiene and appearance while chatting, gossiping, and snacking on food.

Warm and hot water was obtained by means of subterranean conduits of air that were heated by firewood-burning boilers. The Arab baths were supported by the public, however during early Christian rule, before most of them were banned and ultimately destroyed, a tax was implemented in the form of a set admission fee that was required to gain entry. Some bath houses were luxurious and others were humble; in either case, they were modeled after those of the Romans that contained three separate rooms.

The client was first greeted by an attendant inside the reception area or room that was known as *bayt al-musalaj*. The first was the cold room or *bayt al-barid*, where the client left clothing behind and collected towels and wooden slippers. Massages were available in this room before and after the bath. Next was the warm room or *bayt al-wastani* that was used for cleansing impurities, and finally the hot room or *bayt as-sajun* that also contained a large bath or small pool. Within these establishments one could choose to be pampered by a perfumist, masseuse, barber, manicurist, cosmetician, or hairdresser.

During the 10th century, it became fashionable for the men to wear their hair short as opposed to their previous longer styles similar to that of the Visigoths. The women were fond of adorning their eyes with *al-kohl* (kohl) while *al-heña* (henna) was used to color their nails; and for lipstick, the shell of a walnut was applied to tint the lips and gums. The Muslims have always been quite fond of perfumes and aromatic oils; among the most popular were scents of violet, jasmine, musk, almond, narcissus, rose, and water lily.

These products and others could easily be found in the *zoco* (derived from *as-suq* or "the market"). The market was a place for socializing as well as for business transactions and commerce. Throughout al-Andalus, Mayrit became known for producing quality products; these markets or bazaars grew, initially providing goods to the military population and later functioning as general markets with shoemakers, craftsmen, fabric makers, potters, and bakers.

Just as the bath houses were modeled after the Roman bath houses, the homes were modeled after the Roman houses that were constructed in quadrangular shapes. In an average Moorish house, you would enter through the *zaguán* or vestibule where access to the patio was gained through a zigzag pattern to ensure privacy from the street. Inside you would find at least one bedroom and a room reserved for the women of the household to congregate in, known as a harem or *harén* (from the Arabic *haram*, meaning "prohibited" or "forbidden"). Windows opened up in the house onto an interior patio rather than to the street, adding increased privacy while allowing light and fresh air to circulate. Rather than doors, the Moors made do with curtains of fabric or esparto grass in the interior of the house. The floors were covered with earth and those families of better means layered it with lavish carpets.

In excavations that took place at Plaza de la Armería by the royal palace of Madrid between 1999 and 2007, the remains of a total of six houses were discovered. These 10th century homes were comprised of a patio or small courtyard with a cistern in the center and a basement or cellar. The particular dwellings remained unchanged until the 14th century when they were destroyed while the land was filled and leveled for expansion projects. Over the centuries, the Moorish wall was also demolished or destroyed in parts in order to use the material to build foundations, homes, buildings, and for the expansion of streets.

Notable Men

Mayrit had its own governor that was appointed by the Caliphate of Córdoba. The *Anonymous Chronicles of Abd ar-Rahman III* provides a list of names of influential men including such governors who were either from Mayrit or spent most of their lives here.

The earliest mention of a governor is dated to 870/871; *Ubayd Allah ibn Salim* is believed to have been the first to hold the title of Governor of Mayrit. *Abd Allah ibn Muhammad ibn Ubayd Allah* was governor of Madrid in 929 and belonged to the prominent Berber family of the *Banu Salim* (or *Zulema*). Numerous governors of Mayrit during the Umayyad period included members of this well-known family that settled between Medinaceli and Mayrit during the 9th and 10th centuries. Another notable family member was the brilliant scientist and professor of philosophy, *Said ibn Salim*, who was born in Mayrit during 906 and taught in Toledo.

In the year 929, *Abd Allah ibn Muhammad ibn Ubayd Allah* governed in Mayrit. *Ahmad ibn Abd Allah ibn Yahya al-Layti* also served as governor and was recognized as a learned man of science, philology, and poetry, who died shortly after being ambushed by Christian troops in 936. Governor *Ahmad ibn Abd Allah ibn Abi Isa* took his place in 937.

Another prominent family from Mayrit was the *Banu al-Hayy*, whose many family members served in chief positions throughout al-Andalus. *Abu al-Hasan Abd ar-Rahman ibn Isa ibn al-Hayy* was born in 1080 and served as a judicial consultant and judge of Ronda and Málaga. His son, *Abu al-Abbas Yahya ibn Abd ar-Rahman ibn Isa ibn al-Hayy*, was born in 1126 and served as *qadí* or judge of Murcia, Jaén, Granada, and Córdoba where he died in 1208. Another member of the Banu al-Hayy family of Mayrit was *Abu al-Abbas Yahya ibn Muhammad ibn Faray ibn Fath*. He was regarded as an expert in literature and master of the Arabic language who spent most of his life in Mayrit and died in Córdoba in 1121.

Other notable men of Mayrit include *Abu Muhammad Abd Allah ibn Sa'id al-Mayriti*, a traditionalist who taught mostly in Toledo and Córdoba until he died around the year 1000. *Abu Nasr Harun ibn Musa ibn Salih ibn Yandal al-Qaysi* was a cultured man of literature and grammar who dedicated himself to teaching. *Abu Utman Sa'id ibn Salim al-Mayriti* was an honorable and compassionate man who also dedicated himself to teaching specializing in the subjects of religious and military life in Mayrit, where he died in 986. *Abu al-Mutarrif 'Abd ar-Rahman ibn Abd Allah ibn Hammad* was born in 939 into another illustrious family from Mayrit, the *Banu Hammad*. Ibn Hammad was a well-known philosopher and historian described as being a "virtuous, devout, chaste, and humble man" who died in 1016. His son, born in 1004, was *Abu Ya'qub Yusuf ibn Abd ar-Rahman ibn Hammad*; he worked as a lawyer and an expert calligraphist. Ibn Hammad was a well-read man who specialized in the division of inheritances; he died in Mayrit in 1081.

One of the most brilliant Muslim scholars to emerge from Mayrit was *Máslama ibn Ahmad Al-Mayriti*, who was born c. 950. "Al-Mayriti" means "the Madridian" or "Madrilenian", both meaning "the man from Madrid," as this is where he was born. Other examples of this appellation were "*Al-Yayyani*" (from Jaén), "*Al-Qurtubi*" (from Córdoba), *at-Tulaytuli* (from Toledo), *at-Talamanki* (from Talamanca), *al-Balansi* (from Valencia), *as-Saraqusti* (from Zaragoza), *al-Yilliqi* (from Galicia) and *al-Ifriki* (from Africa.)

Al-Mayriti was a leader among those in his field and is referred to as the "Euclid of Spain." His full name was *Abu al-Qasim Máslama Ibn Ahmed al-Faradi al-Hasib al-Qurtubi al-Mayriti*. Al-Mayriti was the most prominent mathematician and astronomer/astrologer of al-Andalus and, according *Ibn Hazm*, an 11ᵗʰ century theologian, historian, and philosopher from Córdoba, there was no equal in his field. *Ibn Jaldun*, a 14ᵗʰ century astronomer, historian, theologian, mathematician, and philosopher from North Africa stated that "the most famous minds of these sciences were Yabir ibn Hayyan in the Orient, and the Andalusí Máslama ibn Ahmed al-Mayriti."

Although al-Mayriti was born in Madrid, he lived and taught for most of his life in Córdoba. His career included authoring many works on the subjects of mathematics, geometry, and astronomy. He taught philosophy, translated and perfected the astrolabe of *Batlomius* (Ptolemy) and his astronomical maps. With his daughter *Fatima*, he revised and expanded the Astronomical Tables of Persian master scientist and mathematician *al-Kwarizmi* (b. 780) while adapting these tables to the meridian of Córdoba.

Al-Mayriti's daughter, *Fatima al-Mayriti*, became a well-respected and brilliant astronomer and mathematician in her own right. Fatima not only collaborated with her father, correcting and editing astronomical tables, but also wrote several works that are known as "The Corrections by Fatima." The collection of manuscripts in the library in the Monastery of El Escorial in Madrid houses the father-daughter collaboration titled "Tratado del Astrolabio" that deals with the use of astrolabes. Fatima is known in history as the first female astronomer/astrologer (regarded as one profession) of al-Andalus.

Her father Al-Mayriti is credited with bringing the concept of zero to al-Andalus. He also wrote a large number of books sharing and demonstrating his extensive knowledge and wisdom in such subjects as alchemy, magic, and talismans, the most famous being *"Rutbat al-Hakim"*(Rank of the Wise.) Al-Mayriti considered alchemy and magic the products of philosophy and science, and thought that those who believed otherwise would never be able to achieve the fruits of the learning of philosophy. He was also quite well-known for his astrological predictions as he served as the personal astrologer to General *Abu Aamir Muhammad Ibn Abdullah Ibn Abi Amir* (938–1002), who is better known by the title he claimed for himself in 981 of *al-Mansur*, meaning "the Victorious." *Almanzor*, as he is known in Castilian, did not initiate any military campaign without the stellar advice and wisdom of Al-Mayriti, who carefully analyzed the planetary alignments before the General began his military expeditions. In the year 977, Al-Mansur, known as a ruthless leader, chose Mayrit as the operational base and starting point of his military campaigns against the Christian troops. His victories over the Christians are over 50 in number and include the taking of such cities as Barcelona, Coimbra, León, Zamora, and Santiago de Compostela.

Although Al-Mayriti and Fatima were born in Madrid, they spent most of their lives at the palatial city built by Abd ar-Rahman III of *Madinat Az-Zahra* in Córdoba, where those of higher minds and culture united to share ideas and expand knowledge. Al-Mansur built another smaller palatial residence, also on the outskirts of Córdoba, that he named *Madinat az-Zahira*.

It was during the rule of Abd ar-Rahman III that Mayrit's military character began to fade as it developed into the city known as *Medina Mayrit*. Also at this time, al-Andalus experienced its Golden Age as Córdoba was then one of the most important Islamic cultural capitals of the world. It has been estimated that during the 9th and 10th century, Córdoba had over 800,000 inhabitants with more than 300 mosques.

While the rest of Europe struggled through the Dark Ages, the most brilliant minds from afar came together in the capital of al-Andalus to study and further the fields of medicine, mathematics, geography, astronomy, philosophy, chemistry, zoology, and history, supplying Europe with a wealth of knowledge. Together, the Muslims, the Christians, and the Jews collaborated in the recompilation and translation of many classic works.

It was at this time when the finest poetry was also produced in al-Andalus. *Abu uhammad Ali ibn Hazm* (994–1064), known in Castilian as *Abenhazam*, was one of the great poets of his time. Ibn Hazm was born to a Muladí family in Córdoba and authored over 400 manuscripts, his most famous work being *Tauq al-Hamamah*

(*The Necklace of the Dove*) that is regarded as one of the finest works of romantic poetry and prose written in Arabic.

In Córdoba Al-Mayriti founded a school where scholars and scientists gathered. One of the students who attended this school was *Ibrahim ibn Sa'id al-Sahli al-Wazzan*, who constructed spherical astrolabes or celestial globes and wrote the first treatise on this subject in al-Andalus during the 11th century.

Many of the works of al-Mayriti, translated into Latin by Mozárabic monks, eventually passed into the Christian West, greatly contributing to the universal study of these sciences. Al-Mayriti may have also founded another school or learning center in Mayrit, focusing on the subjects of astronomy and mathematics; it is said to have appeared in documents dated to 1004. Little if any information is available on this institution of learning; if it existed, it was not as large or renowned as the often-cited centers of Córdoba and Toledo.

One of the brilliant minds of Mayrit, poet Lope de Vega (1562–1635), native of Madrid wrote,

> *la llamaron Madrid, que significa*
> *madre de todas ciencias, en su lengua,*
> *o porque aquí las enseñaban ellos*
> *o porque el cielo entonces, como ahora*
> *producía tan fértiles ingenios. . .*

> *they named her Madrid, which means*
> *mother of all sciences, in their language,*
> *whether because here is where they studied them*
> *or because heaven then, like now,*
> *produced such fertile talents...*

The Taifa Period

The total demise of the Caliphate of Córdoba took place by about 1035, and it led to the emergence of the fragmented rule of the Taifa kings (*Mûluk al-Tawâ'if*). The Taifas were Muslim kingdoms or regional states of independent rule, each with its own king, that arose within al-Andalus once the Umayyad Empire crumbled. The Taifa kingdoms were many and Seville was regarded as its cultural capital while Zaragoza, Valencia, and Toledo were most powerful.

After the demise of the Umayyad Caliphate, Mayrit was incorporated into the Taifa Kingdom of Toledo. This kingdom not only comprised the actual province of Toledo, Madrid, Guadalajara, Ciudad Real, and Cuenca, but parts of Ávila, Albacete, Cáceres and Badajoz as well. As a result of these new, as yet unorganized rulers, tensions increased that helped the Christian troops conquer this territory.

It was the year 1047 when Fernando I, King of Castile, conquered Mayrit and its surroundings, only to abandon it and return the city back to the Taifa Ruler of Toledo, *Al-Ma'mun*, in exchange for payment of a small tribute. Just as Ramiro II conquered Mayrit in 932 and immediately abandoned it, history repeated itself a little over a century after.

During the mid 11th century, as the Christian kingdom expanded, the desperate Moors reluctantly called upon the Almorávides for help. The Almorávides (derived from *al-murabitun*, meaning "the people of the Ribat") were a fanatic Berber dynasty and warriors from the Atlas Mountains who ruled in North Africa. However, in 1085, Alfonso VI conquered Toledo (and Madrid) with the help of Muslim governor and last Taifa king of Toledo, *al-Qadir*, who in turn was given rulership of Valencia. Historians do not agree on the details and many believe that Madrid was conquered before Toledo in 1083. Regardless, along with Madrid fell the other cities in the Middle March including Guadalajara, Talamanca, and Talavera.

After the loss of Madrid and Toledo and the deterioration of the weak empire of the Taifa kings, the Christians armies of Alfonso VI gained in strength and numbers. The Moors were given the choice of accepting their new rulers or leaving their homes. Many departed, mainly those of better means, and moved to the south, particularly to Moorish Granada where many Muslims remained. The poorer or manual labor classes, farmers and artisans, could not risk or afford to move and therefore remained in Christian Madrid.

The entry of Alfonso VI into the city marked the end of Medina Mayrit, as it fell into Christian hands. Alfonso VI fervently tried to repopulate the city with Christian Mozárabes, whom he brought over from Córdoba, in hopes that the Muslim population would eventually dissipate.

Virgen de la Almudena

When Alfonso VI and his men marched into Madrid in a procession on November 9, 1085, he passed by Cuesta de la Vega. According to legend, a part of the Muslim wall crumbled and collapsed, revealing a holy wooden image with two lit candles, believed to have been concealed for three centuries by the Visigoths. However, the Muslim wall was not constructed until the second half of the 10th century. Furthermore, if the sculpture was actually hidden in the Muslim wall, it would not have been necessary to go to such lengths as the Moors allowed the Christians to maintain their religion with their churches outside of the walled Medina during their rule and there would have been no need to hide the sculpture.

The holy image was brought to the Iberian Peninsula in the year 38 ADE by the apostle Santiago (Saint James) when he arrived with the purpose of spreading the word of Christianity to the region. As the legend goes, when Santiago was visiting the small village that was then Madrid, he left behind the wooden image of the Virgin that he had brought with him from Jerusalem with a trusted disciple. (Other accounts indicate that the sacred image was brought to Madrid by Saint Calógero, disciple of Saint James.) According to legend, the carved image was sculpted by Saint Nicodemus and hand painted by Saint. Luke. The cult of the apostle of Santiago is based in Santiago de Compostela in Galicia, where his remains were believed to have been found.

During the 11th century, the holy image may have originally been discovered in the vicinity of the future wall, near a wheat depot or *almudín* nearby, and for this reason it is known as *Virgen de la Almudena*. Of course it is more likely that the image may have been concealed within the Muslim wall by Christian soldiers under the order of Alfonso VI as he strategically planned his public "discovery."

Once miraculously revealed, the sacred image was brought to be venerated at the nearby church of Santa Maria, where the main mosque once stood. The mosque, built during the rule of Abd ar-Rahman III, was precisely situated where today we find no. 88 c/ Mayor and the corner of c/ Bailén, where a Visigoth and Roman temple likely stood before.

To this day, the citizens of Madrid have a great devotion for their patroness, La Virgen de la Almudena. The sculpture that you see today in the cathedral of the same name was installed in 1941, replacing one that had been destroyed during the civil war. This previous sculpture, however, was not the original, which is believed to have been lost in a fire during the 15th century. Legend has it that when the Cathedral was being built, a small pouch was found inside the head of the wooden sculpture containing gold dust and ashes. It is believed that this was the residue of the original carved image of the Virgen de la Almudena. The inscription below her representation in the Cathedral today reads:

> *Imagen de Maria Santísima de la Almudena. Ocultada en este sitio en el año 712 y descubierta milagrosamente el de 1085.*

> Image of Maria Santísima de la Almudena. Hidden in this place in the year 712 and miraculously discovered in 1085.

The discovery of the image of Santa Maria de la Almudena marked the "liberation" of the Muslim population of Mayrit as Alfonso VI conquered the territory, incorporating it into his Christian Kingdom and appointing Toledo as his new capital. The loss of Madrid and Toledo was to have a devastating effect upon Moorish Spain, while Christian armies were rapidly gaining control of the entire land. Although some Muslims remained after the conquest, it was ultimately the definite demise of Medina Mayrit.

5. Magerit (Christian Madrid)

Three years after the death of Almorávide king and co-founder of Marrakech, *Yusuf ibn Tashufin* (r. 1061–1106), his son and successor *Ali ibn Yusuf ibn Tashufin* (r. 1107–1143), with his army, set up camp directly below the Alcázar of Madrid. The area below the Sabatini Gardens of the royal palace is named *Campo del Moro* (Encampment of the Moor) to commemorate this military event. The year was 1109, when Alfonso VI died, and although the Almorávides managed to destroy much of Madrid and the surrounding areas of Talavera and Guadalajara, they failed to conquer it outright.

The Almorávides were defeated by the *Almohad* Berber tribe in 1147, when they captured their capital of Marrakech. The last of the Almorávides, the *Banu Ghaniya*, fled to the Balearic Islands, which they had been ruling since 1126, and they remained in power here until the early 13th century. Madrid was never conquered by the Moors again; however, in the year 1198, Almohad Caliph *Abu Yusuf Ya'qub al-Mansur* also encamped at Campo del Moro only to abandon the area a few days later. The rule of the Almohades (derived from *al-muwahhidun* and translated as "the Unitarians") was short lived as they were defeated by Alfonso VIII in the battle of *Las Navas de Tolosa* in the province of Jaén during the summer of 1212.

Campo del Moro

In the 12th century mosques began to be converted into churches. The main mosque of Medina Mayrit became the Church of *Santa Maria de la Almudena* that stood until 1870. Another mosque is believed to have been situated where the church of San Nicolás stands today in old Madrid.

During the early 13th century, Madrid began to expand outside its walled limits. The wall known as the second or Christian wall was constructed to incorporate the arrabales or suburbs that were growing and being developed outside to the east of the walled premises. Some historians subscribe to the theory that construction of this second wall actually begun under the orders of Abd ar-Rahman III, the first Caliph of Córdoba, after the destruction of Madrid by Ramiro II of León between the years 932 and 950.

The Christian Wall

Archaeological findings have revealed that the Moorish wall and the Christian wall co-existed in Madrid. Remains of this second wall, of material different to that used in the Muslim wall, were discovered in 1983 during an excavation and although both originally were thought to have been built by the Moors, it is now confirmed that the second wall dates to the Christian period.

The first time this wall was documented is in the *Fuero de Madrid* (Royal Charter of Madrid) of 1202, detailing the codified local customs sanctioned by King Alfonso VIII. To trace the outline of the Christian wall that also incorporated the three gates of the Muslim wall, one begins at the Alcázar, continuing south to Cuesta de la Vega, c/ de Segovia, Cuesta de los Ciegos, c/ de Yeseros, c/ de la Morería, and c/ Angosta de los Mancebos to Puerta de Moros. From here, continue along c/ del Almendro, c/ de la Cava Baja to Puerta Cerrada, c/ de los Cuchilleros, and Cava de San Miguel to Puerta de Guadalajara on c/ Mayor, continue on c/ del Espejo, c/ Mesón de Paños, c/ Escalinata, and finally Plaza Isabel II, which brings you back to the starting point of the Alcázar. (Let the reader be aware that the wall did not precisely pass along these streets per se, but rather through the blocks of houses on the streets that stand here today.)

The largest vestiges of the second wall can be seen between the streets and plazas of Angosta de los Mancebos and Yeseros; Escalinata and Espejo; del Almendro and Cava Baja as well as Don Pedro, Meson de Paños, Plaza de Isabel II, and Plaza de Oriente.

More precisely, on numbers 3 and 5 of c/ Angosta de los Mancebos, you can appreciate a fine close up of the ruins of the Christian wall through the gated fence of the apartment complex. Islamic remains in four excavated silos on this street were discovered here that yielded an abundance of fragments of ceramic material and a scarce amount of glazed ceramics that were dated between the 9th and 11th centuries. Also unearthed were two miniature statues believed to have been game pieces in the form of a black pawn and a tower. Ceramics dated to the Roman Era were also discovered here and in 1984, remains in the form of bones and additional ceramics dated to the Bronze Age were also unearthed at this location.

At number 9, 11, and 13 of c/ de la Escalinata you can observe the vestiges of a semi-circular tower of the Christian wall that was flawlessly incorporated into the building during a creative construction project of the 19th and 20th century. It is the only tower in the city that remains complete and is actually situated on number 12 of c/ del Amendro although visible from c/ de la Escalinata. Also at numbers 15 and 17 of c/ del Almendro are ruins of the Christian wall that can also be seen through a gate.

Escalinata (above) and Almendro (below)

Angosta de los Mancebos

At numbers 10, 15, 22, 24, and 30 of c/ Cava Baja, further remains have been discovered such as fragments of the Christian wall and the base of a semicircular tower. At numbers 2 and 8 to 12 on c/ de Don Pedro a fragment of nearly 100 feet in length of the Christian wall was exposed and at numbers 11, 13, 15 of c/ Mesón de Paños further similar vestiges are revealed; however, these are not in the best of state.

In the year 2000 a section measuring 230 feet was exposed of the Muslim wall between the Cathedral of Almudena and the Plaza de la Armería. The base of a Muslim watchtower known as *Torre de los Huesos* (Tower of the Bones) is exhibited inside an underground parking garage at Plaza de Oriente in front of the Alcázar. Built during the late 11th century, the tower's function was to protect the Christian gate of Puerta de Valnadú. Although it is of Muslim origin, built just before the Christian conquest of Madrid, it was incorporated into the Christian wall as a protective tower. The watchtower received this name as it was situated near the Muslim cemetery named *La Huesa del Raf (the Grave of Raf)* by Puerta de la Xagra and outside the walled area to the north of the city. While this necropolis is mentioned in documents dated to the 11th century, another Muslim cemetery was situated by Puerta de Moros that was mentioned in early 10th century documents. Additional ruins of one of the towers of the Muslim wall known as *Torre de Narigues* are located at building no. 83 on c/ Mayor.

As recently as September 2009, further vestiges of the second wall were discovered during construction work at the Madrid subway or metro station known as Ópera at Plaza de Isabel II. According to a representative of the subway station, these remnants were to be exhibited in the corridors of the metro station in spring of 2011. On number 3 at Plaza de Isabel II, a section of the wall is revealed in the basement of an American restaurant.

At numbers 4 and 6 of Plaza of Puerta Cerrada, ruins of the wall have been discovered in the basement of the bar known a "La Escondida" (The Hidden). Special permission by appointment only is required to view these, the most complete vestiges of the second wall.

Although the Muslim wall had three gates, four gates were incorporated into the larger Christian wall.

Puerta de Guadalajara, situated by Plaza de Herradores, was built during the first half of the 12th century. It was here where the road leading towards Guadalajara commenced; thus the gate's name. First mentioned in the Fuero de Madrid of 1202, this was the main gate, where commercial transactions took place..

Puerta de Moros was the gate used by the Muslims; it faced the road to Toledo. Quintana wrote:

> La Puerta que después se llamo y de presente también se llama, de Moros, porque por esa salían y entraban en el lugar, por la comunicación que tenían con la ciudad de Toledo...

> The gate that was later known as, and is presently called, [Gate] of the Moors, is so named as it was here that the Moors would go out and come back, because of the contact they maintained with the city of Toledo...

Puerta de Moros was situated in the lowest part of Plaza de los Carros facing southeast, where *Plaza del Humilladero* is today, between the streets of Cava Baja and del Almendro. This gate was destroyed in 1412 by the Muslims themselves as a protest against being banned from gathering in the area.

Puerta de Moros was connected to *Puerta Cerrada* (Closed Gate) by c/ del Almendro. Puerta Cerrada is also dated to the second half of the 12th century. The latter is the least documented of the gates of the Christian wall. This gate, originally known as *Puerta de la Culebra* (Gate of the Snake) due to its narrow and winding form, was rife with hidden corners and spots where thieves and robbers were easily able to hide and attack unsuspecting victims. For this reason the gate was eventually shut down and renamed Puerta Cerrada. It is said that the gate once displayed the horrifying image of a snake-like dragon fashioned in granite stone that was placed at the very top. Those who believe that Madrid's origins are Greek argue that the reptile refers to the insignia that Greek soldiers displayed on their coat of arms and flags. During the 16th century, scholars began attributing the reptile to the highly regarded rattlesnake in reference to the Phoenicians as founders of the city. Puerta Cerrada was ultimately destroyed in 1569.

Puerta de Valnadú faced north and was situated at Plaza Isabel II near the public baths that existed on what was the street of *Caños del Peral*. This was the least important of the gates for it was the most difficult to pass through. A little bridge was built in order to provide easier access. Puerta de Valnadú was also known as *Puerta del Diablo* (Gate of the Devil) as it displayed a large stone at the bottom with five holes resembling the impression of a hand, believed by those who are superstitious to be the imprint of the devil himself.

Valnadu

Towards the middle of the 17th century, the Christian wall had all but vanished due to the many homes and buildings that were constructed on both sides of the ramparts. By the 18th century, the four gates of the Christian wall were destroyed and nothing remains save the names of the Plazas Puerta Cerrada and Puerta de Moros.

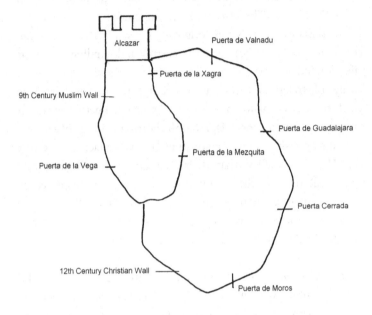

The Mudéjars

During the early years after the Reconquest, the Moors who remained in Christian-ruled Spain became known as *Mudéjars*. The first documented reference that we have of this community is from the Fuero de Madrid of 1202. The Mudéjars of Madrid were mostly farmers, merchants, and artisans who could not afford to relocate. The Mudéjars were industrious and hard working, also excelling as bricklayers, blacksmiths, and *alarifes* or architects. Few samples have survived of Mudéjar architecture in Old Madrid; however, we can still appreciate their work in the Mudéjar towers at Plaza de la Villa and of the churches of San Nicolás and San Pedro.

San Pedro Church

The Mudéjars were allowed to worship according to their Islamic faith and maintain their properties, language, customs, and traditions as long as they paid a special tax. This community was forced to dress in special garments that clearly identified them. The men had to wear a yellow and green hood or cloak with a blue badge or insignia upon their right shoulder and the women had to wear the insignia on their dress. The men were also required to wear their hair and beard in typical Muslim fashion. The Mudéjars were prohibited from owning stores outside their neighborhoods.

By the early 13th century, over half of the Iberian Peninsula had passed onto Christian hands. One by one, the Moorish cities of al-Andalus fell to the Christians; Zaragoza in 1118, Lisbon in 1147, Córdoba in 1236, Valencia in 1238, Jaén 1246, Seville in 1248, Jeréz in 1250, Cádiz in 1262, and so on.

By the second half of the 13th century, the shrinking territory of al-Andalus was ruled by the *Banu Nasr* or *Nasrid* Dynasty of Granada. Their kingdom not only included Granada but most of Almería, Ronda, and Málaga as well.

Malaga

The Nasrids suffered the great loss of both Jaén and Seville to King Fernando; sacrificing these cities in order to secure what was left of Granada.

The Nasrid Dynasty continued to thrive for over two centuries after the fall of its surrounding cities and featured a flourishing silk industry as well as in Mudéjar art and architecture. It was during the Nasrid Dynasty that construction of the magnificent fortress and palace of the Alhambra in Granada began.

Alhambra

The Alhambra was built over a course of 150 years; it was designed to impress, protect, and intimidate; and it was unlike anything that existed in Europe at this time.

The Mudéjars resisted in fully adapting to Christianity, as is evident in their texts and manuscripts written in *Aljamia* (Castilian or *Andalusí* Romance language written in Arabic script). Texts written in this manner developed during the 14th century and are known as *Aljamiado*. The Spanish Jews also wrote in Aljamiado style but in their Hebrew script. It was at this time that the Mudéjars began to be considered as "bad Christians" or "secret Muslims." For this reason they were ridiculed and despised for their habits that others regarded as most peculiar, such as abstaining from consuming pork or drinking wine.

In the year 1469, Queen Isabella I of Castile married King Fernando II of Aragón in Valladolid, thus uniting both kingdoms as one. It was not long before they brought the last Muslim stronghold to crumble. Within the Nasrid Kingdom of Granada, Ronda fell to the Christians in 1485, Málaga in 1487, and Almería in 1490.

Almería

The Nasrids, the last of the Muslim families to rule in the Iberian Peninsula, had no choice but to surrender Granada to the King and Queen of Spain on January 2, 1492, when they captured the Alhambra. It is interesting to note that the morning after Granada was taken, the Spanish monarchs dressed themselves in Moorish garb to receive the keys of the city. The ceremony was witnessed by Christopher Columbus during his campaigns to raise finances for his voyages and expeditions.

By the late 15th century, the Muslims who remained in the country were forced to make a decision between staying in their territory and accepting Christianity as their new faith or moving to the south (al-Andalus), where a small population of Muslims remained. The Mudéjars who left were those of better means; they could actually afford to relocate and start over again with a new life. Less affluent Mudéjars such as artisans, farmers, shoemakers, domestic servants, day laborers, bakers, fruit sellers, spice merchants, tailors, pot makers, ship loaders, and gardeners, stayed behind as they had little to lose by remaining.

Plaza Puerta Cerrada

The more affluent Mudéjars began to settle by the *Plaza de Arrabal* (today's Plaza Mayor) and Plaza de Puerta Cerrada. Here, the artisans and those who were better off relocated in the area encompassing c/ de Cuchilleros, a section of c/ de Toledo, and Cava San Miguel. This became known as the *Morería Nueva* or "new Moorish quarter." The less affluent Mudéjars remained in the area of Las Vistillas or San Andrés that became known as the *Morería Vieja* or "old Moorish quarter."

The Morería

After the Reconquest, the Muslims who lived in the old Almudena relocated to the area of San Andrés. This vicinity was mainly comprised of the streets surrounding the Plaza del Alamillo, Plaza de Paja, and Plaza de San Andrés. Here, the Muslims lived by the other side of Las Vistillas, precisely where the Mozárabe Christians had lived earlier in Medina Mayrit. The Christians began to settle and make their homes in the old Muslim suburbs of the old medina. According to archaeological remains, the Morería Vieja prospered at the beginning of the Christian Conquest.

The Morería of Madrid was a maze or labyrinth of winding, twisting, narrow streets and plazas laced with hidden alleyways; an *adarve* or narrow lane led to each of the private homes. However, the Morería was not just a simple neighborhood; it was governed by an institution known as an *aljama*. An Aljama (derived from *al-jama*, translated as "the congregation") was similar to a town council in the self-governing Moorish or Jewish communities of the Morerías and *Juderías* (Jewish neighborhoods), complete with their own judicial system and principal mosque or synagogue.

The Morería was incorporated as part of the walled city by the mid 14th century it was likely separated from both the Christian neighborhoods and the Jewish quarters by additional ramparts. The neighborhood of the old Morería, located around the southwest corner of the city, was documented as far back as 1190. Several poems have been inspired by the Morería; one author was *Emilio Carrere Moreno*, who was born in Madrid in 1881. Here are a few excerpts of "Madrid Morisco" from his book, *Ruta Emocional de Madrid*:

Barrio de la Morería,
patinado de poesía
y ungido de tradición,
con sus casucas judaicas,
con sus leyendas arcaicas
y su honda desolación....

...Desde los remotos siglos
salen rondas de vestiglos
bajo un lúgubre capuz,
cuando ilumina la luna
la vieja plaza moruna,
con su fantástica luz....

Casuchas pobres y feas,
yacijas moras o hebreas
y un silencio funeral;
recodos y encrucijadas,
ventanas siempre cerradas
y áureas piedras patinadas
de una tristeza ancestral.

Quarter of the Morería,
glistening, shimmering in poetry
and anointed by tradition
with its Jewish shacks
with its archaic legends,
and its profound desolation...

...Since distant centuries
emerge hauntings of vestiges
under a mournful cloak,
when illuminated by the Moon
the old Moorish plaza,
with its fantastic light.

Shacks poor and unsightly
graves of Moors and Jews
and a funerary silence;
corners and cross roads,
windows forever closed
and golden shimmering stones
of a desolate ancestry.

The old Muslim quarter was formed by three plazas: Plaza San Andrés, Plaza del Alamillo, and Plaza de la Paja, the last being the commercial center and the most important of the three, where the main market or *zoco* was located. This market continued to thrive after the Reconquest as indicated in the Fuero of Madrid of 1202. You would also find bath houses, workshops, homes, cemeteries, and storehouses that also served as inns (known as *alhondigas*) for out-of-town merchants.

Originally, the Morerías were closed during the evening; however, the *Mudéjars* could freely roam about outside their areas. Christians were not permitted to live in the Morerías nor were Moors allowed to live in the Christian zones. There is evidence that this was not always respected by either community; as an example, the Moors rented homes from Christians in their part of the city and the Christians in turn would often stay at inns or *alhóndigas* within the Morería.

The general Christian population had free access to the Morerías except for Christian officials who could only gain entry with permission, and then only accompanied by the *adelantati*, who served as an elected official, and the *amin* or appointed financial officer of the Aljama.

By the late 15th century, it has been estimated that the Morería of Madrid contained about 50 households; larger than the Morerías of Toledo and Talamanca. During this time, the population of the Morería along with the Christian suburbs increased to about 12, 500 inhabitants. By this time the original area of 9 hectares had expanded to about 35 hectares.

Madrid-born poet Antonio Casero (1874–1936) also wrote about the Morería.

> *...Mora de la cara mora,*
> *mora de la morería,*
> *que por nacer en el moro*
> *naciste en las Vistillas;*
> *mora que vienes al baile*
> *en el disfraz de odalisca,*
> *agarena de la Cava,*
> *mora de la Fuentecilla,*
> *la que ríe cuando hablo*
> *y disimula su risa,*
> *la que en mi quiere mirarse*
> *y por vergüenza no mira,*
> *ay, mora, morita, mora,*
> *mora de jardín, morita!*
> *Si quieres pa tus amores*
> *Un sultán que te distinga,*
> *Ven, que te haré mi sultana,*
> *y te haré mi favorita,...*

Moorish girl with the Moorish face,
Moorish girl of the Morería,
Because she was born a Moor
Was born in las Vistillas;
Moorish girl who comes to the dance
Disguised as an Oriental dancer
Muslim woman from la Cava,
Moorish girl of the Fuentecilla
She who laughs when I speak
And hides her laugh,
She who wants to see herself in me
But out of modesty does not look.
Oh Moorish girl, little Moorish girl, Moorish girl,
Moorish girl of the garden, Moorish girl!
If you desire for your heart

A sultan who appreciates you,
Come, I will make you my sultana,
and I will make you my favorite...

The Jewish Population

During Muslim rule, the Jewish population lived in the area of La Xagra, where the Plaza de Oriente is today. Little is known about these inhabitants of Madrid; however, we know that they were forced to live in their Judería or Jewish neighborhood. After their expulsion in 1492, it is believed that Jewish converts relocated to the area known today as *Lavapiés* by c/ de la Fe. This theory is based upon the remains found in the nearby area on c/ Salitre that were identified as belonging to a Jewish cemetery. The synagogue is believed to have been situated where the 17th century Church of San Lorenzo stands today.

According to more recent studies, the Judería of old Madrid is believed to have been situated very close to the old Alcázar, more precisely between the Plaza de la Armería and Cuesta de la Vega, at least until their massacre during the late 14th century. This new theory is quickly gaining acceptance based on the fact that Lavapiés is situated far from the old Alcázar that served as protection to the Jewish community.

After the Reconquest, many abandoned their homes in southern Spain and migrated to Madrid during the 12th century. Others settled in the northern region of Madrid by Puerta de Valnadú and stayed there at least until the late 14th century. This became known as the *Judería Vieja*. During the late 14th century, the Jews lived in their Juderías and the Mudéjars in their Morerías; both areas were situated within the walled enclosure. However, in 1391, the great destruction and massacre of the larger Juderías of Spain, including that of Madrid, took place and an estimated 50,000 Jews of all ages were killed.

A law dictated in 1481 stated that Jews also had to dress distinctly in order to differentiate themselves from the rest of the population, and like the Mudéjars, had to wear a special marks, such as a half moon, upon on their clothes to distinguish them from the Christians. The Jewish population was also subjected to special taxes, and inhabitants at this time were forced to relocate to the area of c/ Mayor and Cuesta de la Vega that became the *Judería Nueva*.

Many Jewish scholars excelled at translating Arabic works. However, this small community in Madrid primarily dedicated itself to business and commerce, tax collection, administration, economics, and money lending, as well within the leather, cloth, and jewelry industries. Regardless, during the late 15th century, the Jews (and Mudéjars) were prohibited from selling their products. It was decreed that,

> *Ningun judío nin moro, estrangeros nin de la Villa, no tengan tiendas algunas fuera de sus apartamientos, so las penas de la ley de Toledo, salvo los jueves, ques mercado, que qualquier judío e moro puedan sacar tablas a las plazas desta Villa e sus arrabales (...), e que non tengan nin vendan paños nin otras cosas en casas ni en tiendas, guardando la ley de Toledo, salvo los moros que van a labrar a las casas, que puedan comer donde labran, como es costumbre.*

> No Jews nor Moors, nor strangers from outside the city, shall sell their products outside their designated areas, as per the Laws of Toledo, except for Thursdays, when any Jew or Moor may display their tables in the plaza in this city and its arrabales... and that they shall not sell cloth nor other items in their homes nor stores, as per the Law of Toledo, except for the Moors that work in homes and can eat where they work, as is their custom.

After Granada, the last remaining Muslim stronghold of al-Andalus, was conquered by the Catholic monarchs, non-Christians were given four months to convert to Christianity or be permanently expelled from the country. About 300,000 *conversos* (converts) remained in the country; 150,000 were expelled. Two years later, various Jewish men of higher education and noteworthy professions, such as physicians, were welcome to return to Madrid in order to fill the significant void created by their expulsion.

The loss of the clever Jewish scholars and merchants as well as the special technical skills of the Mudéjars was quite a blow, reducing the basic resources of the country. Once the Mudéjars and Jews were expelled from the peninsula with the fall of Granada in 1492, another significant chapter in the history of Spain emerged: the horrific Spanish Inquisition that plagued the country until it was fully abolished in 1834.

By the beginning of the 16th century, the Mudéjars began to lose their collective identity due to the encouragement of mixed marriages. This population was given the option of undergoing baptism and accepting Christianity or leaving the country. The majority of Mudéjars chose to remain and became known as *Moriscos*, having a similar connotation to "Christian Moors." This population was isolated from Muslim life and culture and was subjected to the authority of the Crown alone. Thousands of Moriscos from Granada were forced to relocate to other regions such as *Castile*, the area surrounding Madrid; the Moriscos integrated with others and eventually died out as a people.

During the middle of the 16th century, the Moriscos were somewhat less persecuted than the Jews, but ultimately suffered the same consequences. The demands of the Catholic Church extended to forcing the Moriscos to completely abandon their customs, habits, language, and clothing. Many became victims of persecution, torture, and mass murder. The expulsion of the Jews and the Muslims resulted in the great economic decline and immense loss of higher learning and education in what was once known as the great land of al-Andalus. Once these cultures were removed, the land's prosperity rapidly declined. Their expulsion gravely damaged the economy of Madrid.

In 1609, King Felipe III ordered the final expulsion of the Moriscos as they had not fully assimilated to Christianity. In 1610, an estimated 400 Moriscos from Madrid and over 4,000 more from Toledo were expelled. By 1614, about 300,000 Moriscos are believed to have been expelled from Spain.

In 1561, King Felipe II established the capital of the country in Madrid when he transferred the royal court from Toledo to this more central location. Not only was Madrid ideally located, equidistant to other major cities, but it was better suited than Toledo with its twisting, uphill streets, very cold winters and extremely hot summers. At this time the population of Madrid is believed to have been about 17,000. During the 16th and 17th centuries, Madrid experienced its golden age of literature, and it generated many talented writers, poets, and playwrights. During the early 17th century, the population of Madrid grew to about 100,000, and it nearly doubled by the end of the century. Today, the population of the capital of Spain has been estimated at over 3 million with a Muslim population of approximately 100,000.

6. Moorish Madrid Today

Historical documentation is limited on the subject of Moorish Madrid; however, we do have significant archaeological evidence in the form of underground chambers, wells, and domestic or household goods, as many buildings and homes were destroyed as the city expanded over the centuries. Artifacts from this population have been discovered at Plaza de Oriente, c/ Angosta de los Mancebos, c/ del Almendro, c/ de Segovia, and Plaza de los Carros to name a few, in the form of ceramics, wells containing ancient refuse, or underground water conduits.

However, the most important vestiges of Medina Mayrit can be seen at *Cuesta de la Vega*, for here you will find the ruins of a section of the 9th century Moorish wall known as *Muralla de Madrid* (Wall of Madrid). Standing as the most important Islamic ruins in the province, these are the only visible remains of Medina Mayrit and represent the oldest Muslim wall to be found in the country. As of the 14th century, the wall began to deteriorate along its gates and towers, and so it was repaired. It was preserved until the 16th century, when it was destroyed during construction of new buildings under the reign of Carlos I.

The Muslim Wall

When construction of a garage began in 1953 at the building that is now no. 12 c/ Bailén, two towers and 164 feet of the wall were exposed at the lower parts of the building that once was the *Palacio del Marques de Malpica* (Palace of the Marquis of Malpica). Sadly, parts of the wall were destroyed during this building project; at one point a sign was placed at the entrance of the construction site that read *"cascotes gratis"* (free rubble.)

Wall ruins (above) and Cuesta de la Vega (below)

Moorish Wall at Cuesta de la Vega

This visible fragment of the Muslim wall at Cuesta de la Vega measures roughly 395 feet in length and 26 feet in height with a width or depth of 6 feet. As one of the main entrances to Mayrit, Cuesta de la Vega is located just below the intersection of c/ Mayor and c/ Bailén at the foot of the Almudena Cathedral. These important remnants of the Muslim wall are displayed across the Cathedral at the park named after the founder of the city, *Parque del Emir Mohamed I.*

Parque Emir Mohamed

The park displayed two ceramic memorial tablets dedicated to the Emir that were donated by the Hispanic–Arabic Institute of Culture on the 30th of March in 1987 with the following simple inscription in Spanish on one plaque and Arabic on the other:

> *El Ayuntamiento de Madrid*
> *Al Emir Mohamed I*
>
> *Fundador de la Medina de Madrid*

> The City Hall of Madrid
> To Emir Mohamed I
> Founder of the City of Madrid

The memorial park was restored and greatly transformed by the summer of 2010. The dedicatory plaques are no longer there, but have been replaced by two larger, highly visible, and informative laminated posters with a map detailing Medina Mayrit, the foundations, archaeological discoveries, and the great restoration project. One section reads:

> *El Ayuntamiento de Madrid ha habilitado el entorno de la antigua muralla islámica de la ciudad para facilitar la visita publica y transmitir el significado y el valor de sus restos arqueológicos. El objetivo es que se establezca un contacto enriquecedor entre la sociedad y este valioso bien de su patrimonio histórico...*

> The town council of Madrid has rehabilitated the area around the city's ancient Islamic wall in order to facilitate public visits and to convey the meaning and value of its archaeological relics. The aim is to establish a fruitful connection between society and this valuable asset of patrimonial heritage...

Parque Emir Mohamed

The modern building on c/ Bailén towards the Cuesta de la Vega was constructed between 1958 and 1962, even though the wall of

Madrid had already been declared a Historic Artistic Monument in 1954. Unfortunately, few tourist resources and guides mention this city's oldest vestiges.

Between 1999 and 2000, a fragment of the Muslim wall, about 230 feet in length, was excavated at Plaza de la Armería by the royal palace.

Plaza de la Armería

This important archaeological discovery remains to be studied pending the re-commencement of the excavation. Scholars believe that this section may correspond to the Puerta de la Xagra. Several other traces of the wall can also be seen nearby but only with special permission, as they are situated on private properties.

The Walking Tour

To trace the outline of the first wall of Mayrit, one should naturally begin at the royal palace, the site of the origins of the foundation of Medina Mayrit where the Alcázar stood, although recently there has been some speculation whether the Moorish Alcázar was actually situated where the *Palacio Real* (royal palace) stands today. There is some archaeological evidence that it may have been located on the site where the Almudena Cathedral presently stands.

During the mid 15th century, an earthquake greatly damaged the Alcázar, and it was reconstructed by Carlos V. In 1734 it was destroyed by a fire that was said to be caused by servants who had not noticed that curtains had ignited. When it was restored in the year 1738, the first stone placed bore a Latin inscription; the phrase "Octavo Kalendas Januarii" refers to Christmas, as it is the 8th (octavo) day counting backward from first day of the succeeding month (kalends) of January.

Aedes Maurorum / Quas Henricus IV Composuit / Carolus V amplifi-cavit/ Philipus III ornavit / Ignis Consumpsit Octavo Kalendas Janu-arii/ MDCCXXXIV /Tándem / Philipus V Spectandas restituit / Ae-ternitate / Anno MDCCXXXVIII

Moorish residence / built by Enrique IV / expanded by Carlos V /adorned by Felipe III / Consumed by fire on Christmas / 1733 / Finally / Felipe V saw it restored / for Eternity / in the Year 1738

Behind the royal palace lies the historical site of the famous 12th century siege at Campo del Moro. The dedicatory inscription here reads:

> On Christmas Eve in 1734, during the reign of Felipe V, a dreadful fire took place, causing the total destruction of the building.... The Campo del Moro is given this name due to the fact that here in the Middle Ages, Almorávide ruler Ali ibn Yusuf encamped with his followers in 1109 in his attempt to recapture Madrid and its Alcázar (Fortress) from the Christian powers.

Campo del Moro

Today, the royal palace is used for official ceremonies, and functions, as well as visits from heads of state. It boasts 2,800 rooms and is decorated with artwork from Goya and Velázquez among others. When not used for official business, around 50 rooms of the royal palace are open to visitors. It is considered to be the largest palace in Western Europe that receives about a million visitors a year.

Royal palace

At the northern end of the royal palace are the Sabatini Gardens. These royal gardens were designed by an Italian architect during the 18th century, although construction did not begin until the 1930s. The soothing Sabatini Gardens opened to the public in 1978.

Sabatini Gardens

We continue to the Plaza de la Almudena that is situated between the Cathedral and Plaza de la Armería, previously know as *Campo del Rey* (Field of the King). One can easily admire the strategic location of the Almudena and panoramic views of the Sierra.

Plaza de la Almudena

At the intersection of c/ Bailén and c/ Mayor you will arrive at the Almudena Cathedral. Turn by the Cathedral to Cuesta de la Vega where Puerta de la Vega once stood. Here the ruins of the Muslim wall can be appreciated at the park named after the founder of Madrid. Continue your journey on Cuesta de Ramon to c/ Pretil de los Consejos and arrive at the crossroads of c/ del Sacramento and c/ Mayor where the Puerta de la Mezquita once stood.

From here we cross c/ Mayor and continue through c/ de San Nicolas, c/ del Factor, and c/ de Rebeque and back to c/ Bailén. After c/ del Factor you will arrive at c/ de la Almudena as you approach the cathedral. Here lie the ruins of the first Parish of Santa Maria de la Almudena of the 12th century at the spot where the major Mosque of Medina Mayrit once stood. The little church was demolished in 1868 to widen c/ Bailén and to begin construction of the Viaduct. Today, the stone blocks appear to be protected by a metal statue of a modern man as he is posed pondering over the glass-protected ruins. This statue is strategically placed as the ruins are quite easy to miss or walk by. A part of the inscription reads:

> *Esta iglesia fue demolida en el año 1868, con ocasión de unas obras de remodelación de las calles Mayor y Bailén que dieron lugar al trazado de la manzana situada detrás de esta placa. Fue principal parroquia del Madrid medieval y se erigió sobre la mezquita mayor islámica.*

This church was demolished in the year 1868, on the occasion of the remodelling work of the streets Mayor and Bailén that resulted in the outline of the block situated behind this plaque. It was the main parish of medieval Madrid that was raised over the Islamic main mosque.

We end the tracing of the Moorish wall by continuing from c/ Bailén to Plaza de Oriente where the Puerta de Xagra stood taking you back to the starting point of the royal palace and former Alcázar.

Plaza de la Puerta de Moros

Plazas of the Morería

Entrance to the old Morería of Madrid was accessed through Puerta de Moros where the *Plaza de la Puerta de Moros* is today. It was in the surrounding area of this gate where the Mudéjars continued to live after the Reconquest. At this plaza, I took the opportunity to take this photograph at the precise moment that a Muslim woman happened to pass by this plaza.

Another interesting plaza is the *Plaza de Alamillo*, a significant area within the Morería, as it was here where the Muslim court assembled. This is one of the most charming plazas of the city as poet Emilio Carrere wrote;

> *Plazuela del Alamillo:*
> *cuanto te recuerdo yo,*
> *con tus floridas ventanas*
> *todas doradas al sol!*
>
> *...Flores lo mismo que entonces*
> *y el mismo rayo de sol*
> *y otros novios que se dicen*
> *dulces nonadas de amor*
> *en la moruna plazuela...*
>
> Plaza of Alamillo:
> how often I remember you,
> with your floral windows
> all gilded by the sun!...
>
> ...Flowers as they were then
> and the same ray of sun
> and other lovers tell each other
> sweet nothings of love
> in the Moorish plaza...

Plaza del Alamillo

Plaza de la Cebada (Plaza of Barley), by Plaza Puerta de Moros, is dated to the late 15th century. This was the site of a market where barley and grain was bought and sold. The old Muslim necropolis was situated nearby and during the 19th century this plaza was used for public executions.

Plaza de la Villa (Town Plaza or Village Square) off c/ Mayor was once an important Muslim market that persisted and thrived during Christian rule. During the 14th century this market represented the center of the city. It was converted into a square or plaza a century after during the rule of Enrique IV. The Plaza de la Villa was originally known as *Plaza de San Salvador* named after the church that existed at this spot. This square is considered to be the oldest of its kind in the city as it houses a 15th century Mudéjar tower of the home of the distinguished family of the *Lujanes* that is known as the *Torre de los Lujanes* (Lujanes Tower.) Plaza de la Villa is situated halfway between the two main entrances of Medieval Madrid; Puerta de la Vega and Puerta de Guadalajara.

Plaza de la Villa

Before Plaza Mayor became the main plaza of the city, *Plaza de la Cruz Verde* (Plaza of the Green Cross) held this prestigious honour. This plaza was also used by cavalries as a meeting point while they entered the city through the Puerta de Moros. The plaza received its name as a green cross was placed here to indicate the site of an execution during the Spanish Inquisition. Carrere wrote:

> *...Plazuela de la Cruz Verde:*
> *un siniestro*
> *brasero inquisitorial*
> *—coronas y paños negros*
> *procesión de condenados, entrevista*
> *de los cirios al fulgor amarillento...*

> ...Plazuela de la Cruz Verde:
> a sinister
> inquisitorial brazier
> —crowns and black cloths
> A procession of the condemned, questioned
> In the golden glow of the holy candles ...

Plaza de la Cruz Verde

Plaza del Biombo

Plaza de la Cruz Verde is situated halfway up c/ Segovia by Cuesta de los Ciegos (Hill of the Blind.) Cuesta de los Ciegos stretches from c/ Segovia to c/ de la Morería and is composed of 254 steps that are formed in a zigzag pattern. It is said that Saint Francis of Assisi often passed through the hill anointing the blind with special oils and miraculously restored their sight.

Opposite the Church of San Nicolás is the small square known as *Plaza del Biombo* (Plaza of the Folding Screen.) This curious name is due to a large wall that formed a part of a convent that once stood here and reminded the citizens of a large folding screen or panel. Plaza del Biombo was once the location of one of the first Moorish settlements in the area where views of the 12th century San Nicolás church can be appreciated today.

Plaza de los Carros (Plaza of the Wagons) is situated by the church and plaza of San Andrés and Puerta de Moros. It was here where visitors who entered the city through Puerta de Moros stationed their wagons or coaches. At Plaza de los Carros, ceramics were excavated dated to the Bronze Age and the Muslim Era; the most important vestige here is the remnants of a Mayra or Qanat measuring 32 feet in length discovered in 1983 that is dated to the 10th century.

Plaza de los Carros

Nearby at Plaza San Andrés, you can visit the Museo de Orígenes and appreciate the exhibition of the Muslim Era of Madrid and much more. Displayed are various ceramics, cooking utensils, flasks, dishes, large bowls, cups, and lamps dated between the 9th and 11th century. Surgical tools are also exhibited as well as amulets that could have been used as pieces for playing the two most popular games at the time; *ajedrez* (chess) and *alquerque* (checkers), both introduced to Spain by the Moors.

Plaza de la Paja (Plaza of the Straw) near Plaza de Puerta de Moros is situated halfway up *Costanilla de San Andrés*. During Muslim and Christian rule, a great market or zoco was situated here that was first mentioned in the Fuero of Madrid of 1202. This plaza was the site of one of the most spacious and important areas of the villa that served as a medieval commercial center.

Plaza de la Paja

Writer Mesonero Romanos (1803–1882) a native of Madrid, describes this plaza:

> *Esta plazuela, aunque costanera e irregular, es la mas espaciosa en el recinto interior de la antigua villa, y podía ser considerada como la principal de ella, pues sabido es que la que tiene esta categoría, no ex-*

istió hasta el tiempo de don Juan II y eso extramuros de la puerta de Guadalajara...

This plaza, although uphill and irregular, is the most spacious in the interior enclosure of the old town, and could be considered as the main plaza, although it held this category, it did not exist until the times of Juan II and of those suburbs by the Gate of Guadalajara.

Walking through the Morería

One can still appreciate the Moorish essence of the old Muslim quarter of Madrid as its tracing remains today as it was then. Unlike the Muslim wall to trace, this labyrinth of streets and plazas can be tricky and complex. To begin, I chose the fittingly starting point of the Plaza de la Puerta de Moros, gateway to the old Morería of Christian Madrid, that once faced today's Plaza del Humilladero situated between c/ de la Cava Baja and c/ del Almendro.

Fountain Plaza Puerta Moros

From Plaza de Puerta de Moros you can begin to appreciate the winding labyrinth of plazas and charming streets that you will encounter such as Alamillo, del Toro, Angosta de los Mancebos (where a fragment of the Christian wall is visible), Redondilla, Alfonso VI, Cava Baja, Almendro (where additional fragments of the wall can be seen), Yeseros, Granado, and of course, c/ de la Morería.

Calle del Toro

Within the Morería, you can appreciate the superior and distinct Mudéjar architecture by walking up c/ del Nuncio off c/ Segovia, for here you will find the 14th century Mudéjar tower of *Iglesia de San Pedro el Viejo* (Church of Saint Peter the Elder). The church, believed to have been built over the site of a mosque, was declared a National Monument in 1886 and houses the tombs of Kings Alfonso I and Ramiro II. On Costanilla de San Andrés wonderful views of the tower can be seen.

San Pedro Church

From c/ Segovia, where the stream of San Pedro once flowed, take a moment to appreciate the historic coat of arms on a building façade where the 17th century *Casa del Pastor* (House of the Shepherd) once stood. Situated today at no. 21 c/ Segovia facing the Viaduct, is the oldest coat of arms of Madrid dated to the 17th century.

Casa del Pastor

The Casa del Pastor was once the home of an elderly clergyman named José whom upon his death-bed declared that the first person to enter Madrid by Puerta de la Vega during the first sunrise after his death would inherit his property. The morning after he died, a shepherd happened to be the first to pass by with his flock and thus inherited the house, hence its name. What is further interesting is that this particular shepherd once provided food and shelter to José who as a younger man, experienced tribulations during the Inquisition. The Casa del Pastor served as the first Town Hall of Madrid and Toledo. The building was demolished in 1972.

From c/ Segovia, head back to c/ Bailén and east on c/ Mayor until you arrive at c/ de San Nicolás where you will find the oldest church in Madrid, *San Nicolás de los Servitas*. The church is dated to the 15th century; however, the Mudéjar bell tower was built during the 12ᵗʰ century. It is believed that the tower was once an *alminar* or minaret of a mosque that stood at this very spot.

San Nicolas

A plaque here reads:

C a m p a n a r i o Mudéjar posible- mente Arabe en su origen; el cam- panario actual de estilo Mudéjar es el elemento mas antiguo original al todo el complejo arquitectural de la primitiva par- roquia de San Nicolás. El cam- panario perdió su cubierta original de 4 vertientes y tejas árabe y fue reemplazado por el actual parte de estilo herrería.

A Mudéjar bell tower, possibly of Arab origin; the existing Mu- déjar-style bell tower is the oldest section of the entire archi- tectural complex of the ancient parish church of San Nicolás. The bell tower lost its original 4-sided sloped covering of Arabic tiles and was replaced by the current ironwork.

Return to c/ Mayor and continue east on to Puerta del Sol; it is a lovely way to wind up the journey and take a much deserved rest. We now end our walking tour of Medina Mayrit and the Morería as we shall now explore Toledo of yesterday and today.

7. Toledo Yesterday and Today

Abu Abd Allah Muhammad Al Idrisi (1099–1166) excelled as a Muslim botanist, geographer, and cartographer born in the Spanish North African enclave of Ceuta. Al Idrisi's maps were frequently consulted throughout Europe by sailors and navigators, including Christopher Columbus. Although Madrid and Toledo were already under Christian rule, Al Idrisi also wrote much about al-Andalus during his time. He praises Toledo as "a well-defended citadel with fine ramparts that were situated in a superb strategic location dotted with fine estates." Al Idrisi's name lives on in an airport named after him in the northern Moroccan port city of Al Hoceima as well as a nieghbourhood in Baghdad.

Algerian-born scholar, historian, and author of the famed "Mohammedan Dynasties of Spain", *Ahmed ibn Muhammad al-Makkari* (c.1591–1632) is often described as the last great historian of the Moors of al-Andalus. He too praises Toledo, describing it as "one of the great cities belonging to the central division."

James A. Michener honors Toledo in his work, *Iberia; Spanish Travels and Reflections*, describing it as "a bejeweled museum set within walls, a glorious monument and the spiritual capital of Spain."

Throughout history, Toledo has been of major interest to con-querors. As a significant Celtiberian settlement, it is first mentioned in documents dated to 192 BCE when conquered by the Romans. First century BCE Roman historian *Titus Livius* wrote:

> *Toletum, ibi parva urbis erat, sed loco munito.*

> Toledo is a minor city, but fortified in position.

The Visigoths selected Toledo as their capital and the Moors as well established it as their capital of the Middle March. During Muslim rule Toledo was known as both *Tulaytulah* and *Madinat al-Mûluk* (City of Kings) as it was here where the court of over 70 rul-ers assembled.

When Berber officer Tariq ibn Ziyad conquered the town in 714, nearly 400 years of Muslim rule followed. However, the Chris-tian Mozárabes of Visigoth ancestry were constantly struggling to break free from the ties held with the Muslim government in Cór-doba. As a result, the Mozárabes of Toledo were severely punished and in the year 797 the horrifying *Jornada del Foso* or "Day of the Pit" took place.

Al-Hakam I (r. 796–822), the Emir of Córdoba, appointed Mu-ladí *Amrús ibn Yusuf al-Muwalad* as governor of Toledo. The Emir's mission was to control the recurring problems with the Mozárabes and Muladíes that made up most of the population of Toledo dur-ing the 9th and 10th centuries. The newly appointed governor devised a plan and ordered the excavation of a huge pit inside his palace where he would host a proposed banquet.

Ibn Yusuf asked the Emir to send forth more troops and under the guise of a special dinner, he invited the soldiers to his palace (other accounts tell of the unsuspecting victims to be rebels and not soldiers.) The governor callously installed executioners at the doors of the palace and as the guests arrived one by one, they were immediately decapitated with their bodies thrown inside the pit. It is said that 5300 men were slaughtered that night. Al-Hakam's young son, the future Emir Abd ar-Rahman II, who witnessed the atrocity, was so affected by it that he suffered a nervous twitch in his eye for the remainder of his life.

This brutal act served to intimidate and quiet the citizens of Toledo somewhat; however, more rebellions did take place, such as one that started in 811 that lasted eight years. Frequent upheavals persisted against the rulers of Córdoba and the Toledans formed an alliance with the Christians in 845, only to be defeated by Emir Muhammad I a few years later.

In the year 1082, the citizens of Toledo once again revolted against the governor, *Al-Qadir* and the Caliphate of Córdoba. Al-Qadir, Taifa king of Toledo, was forced to flee the city and find refuge in the Alcázar of Madrid. Three years later, Toledo was captured by Alfonso VI whose success was not achieved as a result of forceful military efforts or clever tactics. It was accomplished by means of a peaceful pact he made with Al-Qadir who helped him conquer Toledo and all its territories including Mayrit. In turn, Al-Qadir was given rulership of Valencia and its corresponding territories. His life ended in 1092 when he was executed after a rebellion that took place in Valencia headed by its chief magistrate, *Ibn Jahhaf,* who took over his position and was ultimately burned alive three years later.

Toledo was not only the capital of the Middle March but became known as "The City of Three Great Cultures" referring to the traditions and contributions here of the Christians, Muslims, and Jews. Toledo experienced its Golden Era between the 12th and 15th centuries when its artistic and cultural atmosphere then surpassed that of anywhere else in the world. For a while in Toledo, Jews, Muslims, and Christians co-habited peacefully in productive harmony, and the city began to gain a reputation of being a scholarly community attracting brilliant minds from neighboring lands. Intellects, scientists, scholars, artists, poets, philosophers, and linguistic experts of widely varying backgrounds flourished in Toledo as it grew into a major cultural and learning center while the rest of the country was experiencing great intolerance and cruelty during the Reconquest Era.

Toledo continued to flourish under Christian rule and from the temporary unification of these three faiths emerged the renowned *Escuela de Traductores* (School of Translators.) This learning institution arose during the 12th and 13th centuries under the rule of *Alfonso X El Sabio* (the Wise), who was a great supporter of higher educa-tion. Here in Toledo, classical Arab, Persian, Hebrew, and Greek works were translated into Latin and Castilian Romance, becoming available to the rest of Europe for the very first time, such as the Koran for example. Other subjects pursued included astronomy, engineering, geography, mathematics, medicine, philosophy, and science as well as works by such great men as Ptolemy, Copernicus, Euclid, Aquinas, Hippocrates, Aristotle, and Abu al-Walid ibn Rushd or *Averroës* as he is known in Latin.

Don Raimundo, archbishop of Toledo during the first half of the 12th century, was a Benedictine monk born in France and one of the principal founders of the Toledo School of Translators. Don Rai-mundo also adapted the tables of the meridian of Toledo to various European cities. One of the most gifted translator and scholar that he recruited for the school was *Gerard de Cremona* (c. 1114–1187) of Northern Italy. Cremona mastered the Arabic language in order to translate into Latin the many great works such as the astronomi-cal studies of Ptolemy that were originally translated from Greek to Arabic. In all it has been estimated that he translated over 70 scientific texts on the subjects of mathematics, philosophy, medi-cine, astronomy and astrology, as well as alchemy and divination. Cremona died in Toledo and is known as the greatest translator of Arabic scientific texts of his time.

The Sites

The majority of travel guides suggest visiting Toledo as a day trip. Although it takes slightly over an hour by bus, a few days is recommended to spend in this majestic medieval town to visit the major historical sites satisfactorily. It would be a pity to miss the breathtaking views of Toledo illuminated at sunset.

In 1986, enchanting and historic Toledo was declared a World Heritage Site by UNESCO. Today, visiting Toledo should be on the itinerary of everyone traveling to Madrid. Often considered an outdoor museum, Toledo in its entirety has been declared a World Heritage Site as "a monument of world interest to humanity."

Mudejar Gate

Located about 45 miles south of Madrid, Toledo, once an important Roman settlement, the capital of Visigoth Spain, and a prosperous Taifa Kingdom of al-Andalus, is a magnificent city that was occupied by the Moors for nearly four centuries. The old quarter maintains it enchanting Moorish ambiance with its colorful squares, decorative patios and courtyards, charming plazas, hidden corners, narrow, cobbled alleys and twisting streets that require an extraordinary acute sense of direction. The winding, narrow streets and alleyways, both uphill and downhill, can only be explored on foot and comfortable footwear is most essential. When visiting Toledo, it is essential to have a good map as well as a great deal of patience as the labyrinth of streets can be quite confusing. It requires persistence to locate the historical landmarks and finding your way around the meandering streets however it can also be quite enjoyable to become lost in the process.

Toletum (Roman and Visigoth Toledo)

Reminders of the Roman Era survive in the ruins of the city that include the protective walls, a water supply system, and a huge circus that held up to 15,000 spectators. According to the inscription at the entrance of the ruins, the circus was built during the 1st century ADE and functioned until the 4th century. Its maximum length measured 1387 feet and its width measured 331 feet. During the beginning of Islamic rule, the northeast section of the circus was used as a Mudéjar cemetery until the 15ᵗʰ century. This structure was the largest of kind during its time and its vestiges reveal Toledo's significance as a major Roman settlement; in fact the city minted its own coins.

Roman Circus

Additional ruins of Roman Toledo include subterranean caverns situated on *c/ San Ginés*. These caverns are found underneath the property where the church of San Ginés once stood that was first mentioned in 1148 and demolished in 1841. These vaults, known today as *La Cueva de Hercules* (The Cave of Hercules) revealed a subterranean storehouse that was constructed over two phases during the Roman period. This is where, according to legend, King Rodrigo broke the 26 locks of the cave and found himself facing a glimpse of his doom rather than precious treasures and the secrets of his wisdom that were believed to have been buried here for centuries. Sadly, the Cave of Hercules is situated on what is now private property and lies in a greatly deteriorated and dangerous state.

Although there are few reminders of Visigoth presence in Toledo, it is their foundation that most of the churches are built upon.

The Gothic Cathedral stands where a Mosque and Visigoth temple once existed. Interestingly, the mass that is celebrated here is one of the few in the world that is still held in the Mozárabic language. Built between the 13th and 15th centuries, the cathedral is one of the largest of its kind and its craftsmanship is often compared to that of the Cathedral of Notre Dame in Paris.

Cathedral of Notre Dame, Paris

The Visigoth Museum known as *Museo de los Concilios y de la Cultura Visigoda* is located inside the 13th century Mudéjar church known as *San Román*. The interior immediately brought to mind visions and memories of the great Mosque in Córdoba with its classic red and white striped horseshoe arches. The tower of the church is dated to 1166 while the rest of the building was constructed during the first half of the 13th century.

Museum gate

The museum houses the 7th century fragments of a Visigoth headstone or memorial tablet as well as votive crowns, gold leaf crosses, manuscript illustrations, carvings, iron daggers, bronze jugs, and jewelry in the form of belt buckles, collars, bronze rings and earrings of the Visigoth Era. Also on display are reproductions dated to 1976 of the exquisite votive crowns and gold crosses known as the *Treasure of Guarrazar*.

According to legend, one night in 1858, a local couple accidentally discovered an ancient tomb that had been unearthed by the waters of a great storm that had just swept the orchards and gardens of Guarrazar in Guadamur, Toledo. Inside the tombs were magnificent bejeweled votive crowns, gilded crosses and pendants that the couple eventually sold to a local jeweler.

The golden crowns were richly set with emeralds, garnets, sapphires, pearls, crystals, and beads; all in all, a combination of superb

Visigoth and Byzantine craftsmanship. As votive crowns, they were intended to be offerings to the church by Visigoth kings, bishops, and noblemen to be displayed and hung above the altar in the chapels. Among these polychrome votive crowns dated to 670 ADE was the largest at nine inches in diameter and over an inch thick, as well as another of the most spectacular crowns of all times: it once belonged to *King Recceswinth* who ruled from 653 to 672 ADE. This particular crown is adorned with 30 sapphires and four pearls, with an inscription reading *Reccesvintus Rex Offeret* ("offering from King Recceswinth").

Guarrazar Crown

A vast collection of Visigoth goldsmith work is also displayed in Paris on the site of 2nd century Roman-Gallo baths inside a 15th century building that has been converted into the *Musée National du Moyen Age* (National Museum of the Middle Ages) also known as *Musée de Cluny.* Inside, on the first floor, you will find a rich display of the authentic Visigoth crowns, pendants, and crosses from Guarrazar as they were originally brought to France to be repaired and restored.

A portion of the treasure is also on display in Madrid at the National Archaeological Museum as well as at the Armería of the royal palace. A plaque inside the museum reads:

> ...quedan hoy tres lotes de joyas que se guardan en el museo parisino de Cluny, aquí en el Palacio Real y en este Mueso Arqueológico. Constituyen la mejor muestra de los orfebrería de la época VI. Destaca la corona ofrecida por el rey Recesvinto (r. 649–672) de cuya diadema, de oro, cuajada del zafiro *y perlas*....

> ...remaining today are three pieces of jewelry that are held in the Paris museum of Cluny, here in the royal palace, and in this Archaeological Museum. These constitute as the finest samples of craftsmanship in jewelry of the 6th century. Emphasized is the crown offered by Visigoth King Recceswinth (649–672) whose diadem is embellished in gold, sapphires and pearls...

In 1921 a robbery took place at the Armería where a crown belonging to Visigoth King *Suinthila* (r. 621–631) and fragments of another were stolen. The perpetrators were apprehended four years later but the treasures have never been recovered.

Recceswinth's successor King *Wamba* (b. 672–680) fortified the town's walls and had the following phrase inscribed upon the marble gate: *Erexit factore, rex inclitus urbem Wamba suoe celebrem praetendens gentis honorem*. This may be translated as, "Builder and engineer, renowned king of this city, Wamba, celebrated by his men as he stands before his honored people."

Tulaytulah (Moorish Toledo)

The heart of Toledo today is the lively triangular *Plaza Zocodover*. Once the home to bullfights and fairs, Plaza de Zocodover was also used in the *"autos de fe"* (edicts of faith) proclamations of the Inquisition where many victims were imprisoned and burned alive here during the late 15th century when the tribunal was held in Toledo. At the Plaza de Zocodover stands a gate that was known during Muslim rule as *Bab al-Yayl* (Horse's Gate) as a cattle and horse market was held here. Today, it is known as *Arco de la Sangre* (Arch of the Blood) in reference to the Blood of Christ.

Today, the Plaza de Zocodover is cheerfully dotted with bars, cafes, restaurants, and shops that are decorated by arcaded buildings, houses, and balconies. One particular amusing name of a street by the busy plaza immediately caught my attention: c/ *Toledo de Ohio.*

Calle Toledo de Ohio

The most important Islamic remnant in Toledo is the small 10th century mosque interestingly known as the *Mezquita del Cristo de la Luz* (Mosque of the Light of Christ.) This building stands as one of the earliest examples of Moorish architecture in Spain. The mosque was built on the site of a small Visigoth church as traces reveal and custom dictated. An Arabic inscription on the main façade enlightens us to its origins:

> In the name of Allah, this Mosque was raised by Ahmad ibn Hadidi using his own funding, requesting spiritual compensation after death for it from Allah, accomplished with the help of Allah, under the direction of Musa ibn'Ali, the architect and with Sa'ada, it was completed during Muharram in the year 390.

(This date in the Islamic calendar corresponds to the period from December 13, 999 to January 11, 1000 ADE.)

Mosque

Little is known about *Ahmad ibn Hadidi*; he was most likely a member of the *Ban al-Haddad*, a prominent and highly influential Toledan family of the Taifa period.

Prior to the Reconquest, the mosque was known as *Masjid Bab-al Mardum*, named after the nearby gate bearing this name. In the year 1186 the little mosque was converted into a chapel or hermitage and renamed *Ermita de la Santa Cruz* (Chapel of the Holy Cross); however, today it is known as the Mezquita del Cristo de la Luz. It was here where the first Christian mass was held after the Reconquest.

Masjid Bab al-Mardum

According to legend, shortly after the Reconquest, a figurine in the image of a crucified Christ hidden in a niche inside the mosque was discovered. This image had been miraculously lit for centuries by an oil lamp. The illuminated concealed image was believed to have been left behind by the Visigoths when the mosque was a tiny Visigoth church or shrine during the reign of *King Athanangild* (554–567 ADE.)

As the legends continue, in the year 1085 when Toledo was conquered by Alfonso VI, the horse which the king triumphantly rode upon as they marched into Toledo suddenly fell to its knees in front of the mosque. The animal refused to budge and all attempts to raise the horse back up were unsuccessful; this was therefore interpreted as a divine sign. Today you will find a small white stone embedded in the sidewalk directly in front of the entrance to the mosque that marks the exact spot where the horse is said to have "kneeled."

White stone at Mosque Bab al-Mardum

The mosque is situated in the oldest area of the town that was once where the wealthiest Muslims resided. It stands as the only Muslim building prior to the Reconquest that remains preserved in the city. Its proximity to the Alcázar reveals its importance during the Muslim era despite its diminutive size. Although it was converted into a church over nine centuries ago, its trademark horseshoe arches and columns of the interior are also reminiscent of the much larger mosque in Córdoba.

Recent discoveries underneath the mosque have revealed an ancient Roman road 16 feet wide with an underground sewer found in the northern terrace of the garden. Also discovered was an apse belonging to the Roman or Visigoth era in the northern section of the mosque as well as traces of a Christian cemetery that existed between the 12ᵗʰ and 15ᵗʰ centuries.

A few steps from the mosque of Bab al-Mardum is the 10ᵗʰ century Muslim gate of the same name that in Castilian is known and pronounced as *Puerta de Valmardón*. This gate stands as the oldest in the city and is also known as *Puerta del Cristo de la Luz* for its proximity to the nearby mosque. Through this gate was the old entrance to the Medina of Moorish Toledo.

Bab al-Mardum

Another small mosque found nearby that was built a little later around 1160 is the *Mezquita de Las Tornerías*, originally known as *Masjid al-Mustimim*. Here, you can observe the remains of a Roman water supply system on the ground level floor.

Only two of the eight synagogues in Toledo from this era remain standing today: *Sinagoga de Santa Maria la Blanca* and *Sinagoga del Transito*. The synagogue of Santa Maria La Blanca is dated to the late 12ᵗʰ century and is considered as one of the finest examples of Mudéjar art in the country. The synagogue of del Transito was built during the 14th century and houses the Museo Sefardi (Sephardic Museum.) Almost all of the original decorations on both Mudéjar-styled synagogues remain as they were.

Tornerias

The Alcázar stands on a site where a Roman and Visigoth palace or fortification once stood atop the highest hill of Toledo. During the 9th century, the Umayyads built their Alcázar here and during the 11th century, it served as the palace of the local Taifa rulers. After the Christian conquest, the Alcázar was among the main residences of the kings of Castile. Of the original structure, nothing has remained as it has been completely rebuilt through the centuries.

Additional Moorish remnants include 11th century Muslim baths situated on c/ del Angel that can only be visited by scheduled tour groups. Of further interest is a large 15th century astrolabe tapestry on display at the *Museo de Santa Cruz*. Toledo was renowned for producing astronomical instruments known as astrolabes or *safiah* that were frequently consulted by astrologers, astronomers, and navigators in their calculations of planetary positions.

Ibrahim ibn Yayha az-Zarqali (1029-1087), known as *Arzachel* in Castilian, was an influential Muslim-Hispano mathematician and astronomer born in Toledo. His successes included simplifying the Hellenic astrolabe that was eventually introduced into Western Europe. Az-Zarqali improved the works from such great men as Ptolemy and Al-Kwarizmi, compiling a series of astronomical tables and observations that were translated into Latin during the 12th century known as the famed "Toledan Tables." The original Arabic version is lost but two Latin versions have survived.

Toledo was also famous for its water-clocks that were introduced into Spain by the Muslims. Az-Zarqali, who has a lunar crater named after him, also constructed large water clocks that were still in use nearly a century after his death.

Another influential man from Toledo was *Ibrahim ibn Said as-Sahali* who also constructed astrolabes during the 11th century. A stunning example of his work is displayed at the Archaeological Museum of Madrid in the form of a bronze plate measuring 9 inches in diameter.

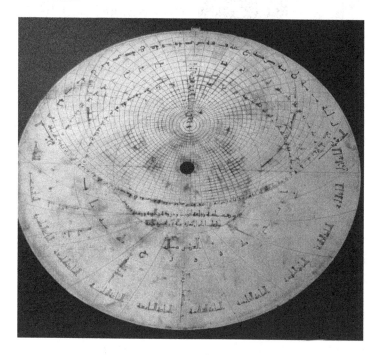

Astrolabe

In certain shops in Toledo, you will find many wonderful metal items such as jewelry and dishes that are inlaid with gold, silver, or copper wire: a technique known as *damascene*. The town has always been quite well-known for its craftsmanship, particularly its metal workers who produced the famous decorative steel swords and knives of various shapes and sizes from the techniques learned from the Moors. The artisans of today still craft the swords and knives using the technology of old. The prized swords of Toledo come in various shapes and sizes and can be found today throughout the many swords shops in the city.

Sword shop

Fifty-four historical reliefs carved during 1495 in the Choir stalls of the Cathedral of Toledo superbly illustrate the detailed scenes of the Catholic conquest of Granada, the last Muslim Kingdom of Spain. Each of these lower choir stalls or seats are carved from walnut wood and are adorned with a different historical battle scene that tell the story of the conquest of the Granada when it once included such cities as Salobreña, Almuñécar, Marbella, Motril, Mijas, Ronda, Malaga, Guadix, Almería, and Mojácar.

The Gates

The entrance to Toledo is through *Puerta Vieja de Bisagra* (the Old Bisagra Gate.) This 10th century Moorish gate was originally known as *Bab-Xagra* (Xagra Gate) and displays its trademark horseshoe arcs and Islamic tower. It is also known as Puerta de Alfonso VI as it was through this gate in 1085 that the king is said to have triumphantly marched into the city.

Puerta Vieja de Bisagra

Today, the main entrance to historic Toledo is the *Puerta Nueva de Bisagra* that is flanked by two gigantic and rounded ornamented towers. Although it is of Moorish origin, the gate was enlarged and reconstructed in 1550 replacing the Puerta Vieja de Bisagra as the main entrance to the city.

Puerta Nueva de Bisagra

Another significant gate is the *Puerta del Sol* (Gate of the Sun) that was constructed by the Knights Templar during the 14th century with origins dating back to the late 10th or early 11th century. This gate received its name as it has the image of a sun and moon inscribed above its horseshoe-shaped door. The 18th century decorative medallion just above the arch displays the ordination of *Saint Ildefonsus*, the patron saint of Toledo.

Puerta del Sol

Of Visigoth descent, Saint Ildefonsus served as the bishop of Toledo from 657 until his death ten years later. The Puerta del Sol stands as a wonderful example of Toledan Mudéjar architecture with its classic arches, high tower, and two adjoining turrets. This gate is often referred to as the finest Mudéjar gate in the country that was once was a main entrance into the city.

Puerta de Cambrón or (Cambrón Gate) is named after the thorny bushes or buckthorns called *cambróneras* that grew nearby. Dated to the 16th century, this gate was completely reconstructed and built over another that was actually built over Visigoth gate. It stands as the only gate in the city that is open to traffic. Puerta de Cambrón is also known as the *Puerta de Los Judíos* or "Gate of the Jews" as it served as the entrance to the old Judería of Toledo according to 12th century documents. It was at this time when the Jewish population of Toledo reached 12,000.

Puerta de Cambrón

The Mudéjar *Puerta de Alarcones* is also believed to have Visigoth origins. This gate was one of the most important gates during Moorish Toledo situated near Puerta del Sol. During the early 13th century, Puerta de Alarcones was known as *Puerta de Mohaguía*.

Puerta de Alarcones

The Bridges

Puente de Alcántara (Alcántara Bridge), dated to the Roman era, was maintained by the Visigoths as mentioned in a poem by Bishop Saint Venantius Fortunatus (c. 535-605.) This bridge on the eastern side of the city was greatly repaired by the Moors during the 9th century; however, its present structure is mostly dated to the 13th and 14th centuries. The Puente de Alcántara stands as the oldest bridge in Toledo. Nearby the Puente de Alcántara, you can visit the ruins of a Roman aqueduct.

Situated at the west end of the bridge is the *Puerta de Alcántara.* Of Moorish origin, this gate was then known as *Bab al-Qantara,* (Gate of the Bridge) however it has been reconstructed during the Christian era.

Alcántara Bridge (above) and Alcántara Bridge II (below)

Puerta de Alcántara

Crossing the Alcántara Bridge we come to the impressive San Servando Castle. This 14th century Mudéjar castle was rebuilt over the site of an Arab fortress that in turn was built over a Visigoth church and Roman fortress. It stands as one of the most important monuments in the province although it has been rebuilt several times over the centuries. Alfonso VI converted it into a monastery in honor of Saint Servando and Saint Germano.

San Servando

The five-arched *Puente de San Martin* (San Martin Bridge) dates back to the late 13th and early 14th centuries; however, it has almost been entirely rebuilt. Originally forming the old defensive wall of Toledo, its construction bears an interesting legend:

San Martin Bridge

In order to construct the much-needed bridge, a local architect or *alarife* was hired to complete the monumental project. During the process, the architect discovered that he had made a grave error in the calculations regarding the cementing of the structure. Fearing that the bridge would collapse when the scaffolding was removed the following morning, the architect went home, and in great despair, unloaded his worries and fears to his wife. The architect's wife knew quite well that if the bridge collapsed, her husband would be blamed and as a result would lose his job, honor, and reputation. She was desperate and devised a plan.

Under the cover of dark, the architect's wife set out to burn the bridge and reduce it to ashes. And indeed, the following morning, nature was blamed for the destructive deed and the need to build the bridge became even more urgent. The alarife was again hired for the job; only this time he fervently corrected his calculations.

As time passed, the wife of the Alarife could no longer live with the guilt of her actions and decided to confess to the Bishop. The Bishop was so impressed by her compassion that he ordered a stone construction to be made in her image to be placed in the central part of the bridge structure.

San Martin Bridge (above) and Baño de la Cava (below)

Near the San Martin Bridge you will find a Mudéjar tower on the left bank of the Tagus River. This tower, known as the *Baño de la*

Cava (Bath of the Cava), is named after the lovely Florinda as it was here where she unknowingly bathed for Visigoth King Rodrigo.

Marzipan

Toledo is also famous for its delicious *marzipan*, a sweet paste of almonds, sugar, and honey: ingredients introduced into al-Andalus by the Moors. This sweet treat can be chocolate-covered or glazed and molded into figurines such as curious shapes of animals or people. Marzipan was documented as being enjoyed by the Mozárabes in the 11th century during Christmas festivities, a Spanish custom that still remains today. Many shops are found throughout historic Toledo that sell marzipan and export it to the rest of the world.

Marzipan

Before we return to explore the many interesting facts about Madrid, I shall close this chapter by including a delicious recipe for Toledan Marzipan:

> Heat one cup of water and two cups of granulated sugar in a saucepan until the sugar dissolves and mixture comes to a boil. Let the mixture boil steadily until the temperature reaches about 230° F degrees using a candy thermometer. Remove from

heat and beat until the mixture turns somewhat cloudy. Stir in three cups of ground almonds, two egg whites slightly beaten and a tablespoon of vanilla extract.

Cook over low heat for about two minutes or until the mixture pulls away from the side of the pan. Sprinkle some of the three to four tablespoons of confectioner's sugar onto a flat surface. Turn mixture onto the surface and knead the mixture until smooth, gradually adding in the remaining sugar. Take small pieces and roll them into whatever shaped desired. Lastly, wrap in foil or wax paper and store in an airtight container.

8. Curious Facts about Madrid

For the reader, I have compiled 25 interesting facts, anecdotes, and legends surrounding Madrid of the past and present.

1. One would hardly expect to appreciate an authentic ancient Egyptian temple in Madrid. However, atop Parque de Rosales in the center of the city by the Plaza de España, stands an Egyptian temple or shrine known as *Templo de Debod*. The structure is magnificently decorated with two narrow gateways surrounded by water that leads up to the temple. It stands as one of the rarest ancient Egyptian monuments that can be visited outside its native land.

Construction of the temple began during the 2nd century BCE as a small chapel dedicated to the great Egyptian deity of *Amen* built under the orders of Nubian King *Adijalamani* (c. 200–180 BCE.) The temple was originally located south of Egypt in the village of Debod in Nubia (Sudan) and was completed by the 4th century BCE during the reign of King *Azakheramón*.

Over the centuries, increasingly rising waters threatened the temple and other ancient Egyptian monuments as they slowly descended into the sea. Between the 1960s and 1970s, Spain assisted in the preservation of such historical ruins during the construction of the Aswan Dam. One of the first monuments to be rescued was the Temple of Debod and so it was offered as a gift to Spain in 1968 by the Egyptian authorities.

Carefully dismantled stone by stone in 1970, the temple was transported upon a ship from Alexandria, Egypt to Valencia, Spain and then by train to Madrid where it was fully reconstructed. Doors were opened to the public in 1972 and today it holds an exhibition of its ancient history and massive reconstruction project.

Templo de Debod

2. Curiously, Madrid was temporarily given to the dethroned king León V (1342–1393) of the Armenian Kingdom of Cilicia. The king, although he apparently resisted, was given rulership of Madrid as a consolation prize for being expelled and losing his kingdom to the Turks. In 1383 León V was named "Lord of Madrid" by Juan I, the King of Castile. León V was not only given the title of Chief Magistrate of Madrid, but of Villareal in the Castilla-La Mancha region, and Andújar in the province of Jaén as well. The foreign ruler also benefited from an income of 150,000 maravedíes to rule these kingdoms.

León V

During his brief rule in Madrid, León V ordered the restoration of the deteriorated towers of the Alcázar and sanctioned the Fuero de Madrid. It is said that he was not particularly fond of Madrid and therefore, León V abandoned his new land for France in 1391 where he died two years later in Paris. His tomb lies in the Basilica of St. Denis along with that of Marie Antoinette and Louis XVI. León V has a street named after him in central Madrid known as *c/ de León V de Armenia* that is situated in the neighborhood of Los Carmenes by c/ Via Carpetana where this author spent most of her summers as a youth.

3. According to legend, a particular 11th century Christian soldier approached the Muslim wall with the intention of taking its inhab-itants by surprise. To the astonishment of all, the soldier began to climb the defensive wall by thrusting his dagger into the narrow seams between the blocks of stones, and he gracefully ascended. So polished and effortless were his moves that those watching nearby compared his agility to the sinuous moves of a cat. For this reason, natives of Madrid enjoy the nickname of *gatos* and *gatas* (cats).

However, natives of Madrid are more properly known today as *Madrileños*. Some Madrileños were known by another name: *Manolos*. *Manolo*, a colloquial derivation of the name *Manuel*, emerged as a name during the 16th century when it was obligatory for Jewish converts who lived in the area of Lavapiés to be baptized by this name. The women became known as *Manolas*, and since the end of the 18th century, from a famous sainete written by Madrileño Ramon de la Cruz (1731–1794), "Manolo" became a synonym for "handsome," "pompous," and "coquettish."

The Manolos and Manolas had their rivals: the *chisperos* and *chulapos*. The Chisperos lived in the area of c/ del Barquillo by the Plaza de las Salezas. The term *chispero* is derived from *chispa*, the Castilian word for "spark," as there were many blacksmith shops located in the area which produced sparks. The *Chulapos* were Madrileños from the Malasaña district that was another neighborhood dotted with blacksmith shops. The term *Chulapo* is derived from *chulo*, that can be translated as a combination of "attractive", "coquettish", "embellished", and "proud". The Chulapo men dressed meticulously well with many adornments such as carnations on their lapels and white handkerchiefs around their necks. Chulapos wore vests or waistcoats with dark, tight-fitting pants, high shoes, and a checkered cap. The women wore a red or white carnation on their hair and a pretty white blouse with a traditional polka-dot skirt and an elaborate fringed shawl over the shoulders.

The Manolos, Chulapos, and Chisperos all fall under the category of natives known as *Castizos*, being a person or thing that is genuine and pure. Those born in the districts of La Latina, Lavapiés, and Chamberí (where the author was born) all proudly claim this title. The term can also be applied to typical costumes, speech, and music that was popular during 19th century Madrid, such as the *Zarzuelas* that were set in a Castizo ambiance that entertained Spanish aristocracy.

4. Madrid has its own form of operetta known as *La Zarzuela*. This musical genre developed during the mid 17th century; however, its golden age was during the second half of the 19th century when it

was revived. Zarzuelas have been described as "Spanish Vaudeville" and are often satirical in nature, consisting of dance, song, and dialogue that was both scripted and improvised.

The Zarzuelas were named after the venue where they were first performed: the *Palacio de la Zarzuela*. This royal summer palace, in the town of Aranjuez near Madrid, served as the hunting lodge and retreat for King Felipe IV. Today, it is one of the residences of the royal family.

5. The Retiro Park is one of the city's favorite public retreats where you can get away from the daily hustle and bustle of downtown Madrid. The park, built during the first half of the 17th century, originally stood as the main gardens of the former royal palace that functioned as a recreation area for nobility. In 1868, the gardens were granted to the citizens of Madrid by Queen Isabella II (1830–1904) when carnivals and festivals were held here; however, there were a few peculiar stipulations that the citizens had to then abide by: The men could only enter the park if their hair was well-groomed and no hats, jackets, capes, or topcoats were permitted. The women had to leave their shawls at the entrance and if they were caught wearing a shawl upon their shoulders or tied at the waist, it was removed by the *Guardas Reales* (Royal Guards).

Retiro

The Retiro Park covers an area of over 120 hectares and is dotted with picturesque gardens, fountains, playgrounds, paths, and over 15,000 trees. There are many activities to choose while at the Retiro Park: row boating on the Great Lake, watch street performers, enjoy live concerts, visit a zoo, relax at an outdoor cafe, jogging, bicycling, cross paths with a roaming peacock, or even have your Tarot cards or palm read.

The Retiro Park also displays impressive works of art and architecture, such as the *Palacio de Cristal* (Crystal Palace) where exotic plants are displayed and protected all year round. This magnificent building, made almost entirely from glass, was built in 1887 to house tropical plants during the cold winter months.

Crystal Palace

6. *Plaza Mayor* served as a small market square during the 15th century that was then known as *Plaza del Arrabal* as it was located in the suburbs or arrabales situated outside the city walls by the Puerta de Guadalajara. During the early 17th century, the plaza was completely reconstructed and enlarged to be used as a court square. San Isidro, Madrid's patron saint was beatified here on the 15th of May in 1620 with a lavish celebration of processions, dancing, and

masquerades that lasted six days. One year after this joyous occasion Rodrigo Calderon, a count and marquis, was beheaded at this very plaza. Calderon was accused of witchcraft and was blamed when Queen Margarita (whose entrance was celebrated at the Plaza Mayor in 1599) died giving birth.

Plaza Mayor

Plaza Mayor has over the centuries been used for such public events as royal entrances, carnivals, bullfights, tournaments, festivals, celebrations, and canonizations, such as San Isidro and four others in 1622. Crowning ceremonies and royal proclamations, as well as grizzly trials and executions during the Spanish Inquisition also took place at the Plaza Mayor. During one particular day up to 110 victims were judged while 21 were burnt alive. Those who lived at the Plaza Mayor during the time of the Inquisition were required to relinquish their balconies as box seats for nobility so they could be "entertained" by the autos de fe (edicts of faith). During the late 18th century, the executions were relocated to the Plaza de la Cebada. The oldest store in the Plaza Mayor dates back to 1790.

Today, this charming and spacious cobblestone plaza is arcaded on its four sides and dotted with souvenir shops, cafes, restaurants, bars, and the selection of nine archways or gates to enter. In the center of the plaza stands the equestrian statue of Madrid-native King Felipe III as the plaza was completed during his reign.

Plaza Mayor II (above) and Plaza Mayor III (below)

The plaque reads:

La reina doña Isabel II, a solicitud del Ayuntamiento de Madrid, mandó colocar en este sitio la estatua del señor rey don Felipe III, hijo de esta villa, que restituyó a ella la corte en 1606, y en 1619 hizo construir esta Plaza Mayor. Año de 1848.

Queen Isabel II, as requested by the Town Council of Madrid, ordered to be placed on this site the statue of King Felipe III, son of this town, who restored her as the capital in 1606, and in 1619 ordered the construction of this Plaza Mayor. Year of 1848.

Along with Felipe III and Queen Isabella II, rulers Fernando VI, Carlos II, and Alfonso XIII were also born in Madrid. Throughout the years, Plaza Mayor has been known by other names such as *Plaza de la Constitución, Plaza Real, Plaza de la República,* and *Plaza de la República Federal.* The plaza is situated in the area known as the *Madrid de los Austrias* (Madrid of the Austrians), a most picturesque and charming area that is also known as *Madrid de los Habsburgs,* or *Hapsburgs.*

Calle del Conde 1952

This historic quarter is named after the Hapsburg Dynasty that ruled in Spain during the 16th and 17th centuries as it was during this period in history that this area of Madrid was developed. King Felipe II was the first Hapsburg to rule Spain in 1554 whose dynasty ended here in 1700.

The Hapsburg Dynasty descended from Carlos I who was also the Roman Emperor Charles V and Archduke of Austria. Carlos I, born and raised in Flanders, was the son of *Juana*

La Loca (Joan the Mad), the only child born to King Fernando and Queen Isabella. Charles V was a teenager when he inherited rulership of Spain and was not in the least interested in his position or the land as is expected of a boy of his age. The Hapsburg Dynasty was instrumental in moving the capital of the Kingdom of Castile from Toledo to Madrid in 1561. However in 1600, the capital was shifted to Valladolid before it was moved back to Madrid in 1606.

During the rule of the Hapsburg Monarchy, tradesmen set up their stores and workshops on particular streets that took the name of their actual profession. For example, in old Madrid today you will still see the streets of *Bordadores* (embroiderers), *Botoneras* (button-makers), *Coloreros* (colorists), *Cuchilleros* (cutlers or knife-makers), Esparteros (esparto grass weavers), *Latoneros* (brass-makers), *Yeseros* (plasterers), as well as the *Plaza de Herradores* (horse-shoe-makers.) The origins of *c/ de los Tintoreros* (dyers) date as far back as the 15th century.

The quarter of Austrian Madrid stretches from the Puerta del Sol to Plaza de Puerta Cerrada, encompassing Plaza Mayor, Plaza de la Villa, c/ de Bailen, c/ Mayor, the Cathedral, Plaza de Oriente, royal palace, Plaza Isabel II, and the streets of Cava Baja and Cuchilleros.

Cuchilleros

Another historic section is known as *Madrid de los Borbones* (Madrid of the Bourbons). At the start of the 18th century, Felipe V became the first Spanish Bourbon ruler. The Bourbons, descendants of a French royal family, ruled here during the 18th century and most of the 19th and 20th centuries continuing to the present.

Historic sites, buildings, fountains, and monuments that were constructed in Madrid during the 18th century reign of the Bourbon Dynasty include the Puerta de Alcalá, Plaza de Colon, Fuente de Cibeles, Fuente de Apolo, Fuente de Neptuno, Parque Retiro, and Paseo del Prado.

7. Where the *Puerta Cerrada* of the Christian wall once stood, known as *Plaza de Puerta Cerrada*, stands a huge mural with the following inscription.

Plaza de la Puerta Cerrada uros

Fui sobre agua edificada, mis muros de fuego son.

Over water I was built, my walls are made of fire.

The reference to water and fire goes back to at least the beginning of the 15th century when it appeared inscribed below the first coat of arms of Madrid. The water referred to here is related to the Qanats or Mayras that were perfected in Mayrit. So important and notable were these subterranean canals that the city took its name from them.

It is generally believed that the fire alludes to the fact that Madrid's first wall was constructed by the Moors with large blocks of flint that were abundant in the area. Flint, a stone that glitters in the sun and can produce sparks, was also used to pave the streets and when horses traveled on these old streets of Madrid, the steel horseshoes created a multitude of sparks. However, the *fire* alluded to in this adage may refer to the relationship between the name of the Roman settlement of *Miacum* by the Manzanares River and the Hebrew term for fire, *miakud*. Incidentally, the name of *Ursaria* (Roman Madrid) is said to be derived from *ur*, another Hebrew word related to fire and flame. This is echoed in an older adage reflecting its origins:

> *Madrid la Osaria, cercada de fuego, fundada sobre agua.*

> Madrid the Osaria, surrounded by fire, founded over water.

Not only are fire and water associated with the name and history of Madrid, but so are the other two ancient elements as well; some believe the name of *Magerit* translates in Arabic as "a place of a soft breeze," an association with the element of air. Madrid was well known for its profusion of pure breezes that came from the Guadarrama Sierra and in 1629 historian and author Jerónimo de la Quintana of Madrid wrote:

> *Los aires que goza Madrid son limpios, puros, y delgados a los que se atribuye la continuación de la salud que tiene.*

> The breezes that Madrid enjoys are clean, pure, and willowy that attribute to the continuation of health it possesses.

In 1623, Madrid-born novelist *Céspedes* and *Meneses* attributes these fresh breezes to the origins of the name of Madrid .

> *Los Moros...la dieron nuevo nombre, y el mismo que hoy conserva, aludiendo la significación del a una de sus mayores excelencias, a sus*

*frescos y saludables aires, porque Madrid no otra cosa significa en su
lengua que lugar de buenos aires: y esto es tan cierto que ni en lo restante
de España, ni aun de la mitad del Orbe, se conoce sitio mas sano.*

The Moors...gave her a new name, the same that is kept today,
referring to the significance of one of its greatest luxuries, its
fresh and healthy breezes, as Madrid signifies nothing in its
language other than place of fine breezes: and this is so certain
that in the rest of Spain, not even in the center of the world, is a
healthier place known.

For the element of earth we have the exceptional clay soil that
produced such fine ceramics in Medina Mayrit that were praised by
geographer Al-Himyari in his *Book of of the Fragrant Garden* during
the 15th century.

8. The *Gran Vía* (Great Road) is downtown Madrid's most important or main street. It stands as a major traffic route and repre-
sents the center of commercial life in the city. The Gran Vía prom-
enade and avenue is packed with restaurants, outdoor cafés, elegant
boutiques, large department stores, music theatres, movie cinemas,
hotels, historic buildings, office building blocks, banks, and souvenir shops.

Gran Vía

Construction of the street began in 1910 and work continued over a space of 21 years. The Gran Vía was designed in order to create a boulevard through the center of the capital linking the eastern and western sections. In order for this to take place, the maze of small twisting lanes that exited in the area were demolished and in total, 14 streets and over 300 homes had to be torn down. Today, as one of the city's landmarks, the avenue lavishly celebrated its 100th anniversary at the time of this writing.

9. One particular street in Madrid, *c/ del León* (Lion Street) has a curious history attached. After the Reconquest and on this very street, a man from far away India displayed a magnificent animal to the public to see for the price of two maravedíes. To the Spaniards, the man caused quite a stir as he was not only wore a colorful kilt, feathered plumes, and a pair of enormous hoop earrings, but was accompanied by a wild and exotic lion that was placed inside a bejeweled cage. This spectacle went on for so long that the street took the beast's name.

Calle del León

Near c/ de León you will find *c/ de Cervantes* named after the famous writer born in Madrid. The city has many streets named after local poets, writers, playwrights, and historians such as *c/ Lope de Vega* (1562–1635), *c/ de Mesonero Romanos* (1831–1861), *c/ de Lopez de Hoyos* (1569–1572), and *c/ de Jerónimo de la Quintana* (1576–1644) to name but a few. Many literary giants and historians were born here as Madrid has always been considered a most literary city.

10. *Puerta del Sol* or "Gate of the Sun" is the main plaza and heart of Madrid, named after a Christian gate that was oriented to the rising sun in the east. First mentioned by this name in 1478, this gate displayed the symbol of the sun at its entrance. By the 17th century, it had acquired a relative amount of importance.

Puerta del Sol

Puerta de Sol is filled with charming bars, restaurants, shops, and boutiques. Until recently, the emblematic bronze sculpture of the bear (*El Oso*) and the Strawberry Tree (*El Madroño*) was situated at the northern end of the square by c/ del Carmen since 1984. In the fall of 2009, the sculpture was relocated to a less crowded location on c/ Alcalá where it originally stood in 1967.

El Madroño

Some believe that Madrid was first known as *Ursaria*, a term possibly derived from the Latin *ursus* meaning "bear," as these animals were abundant in the area. Ptolemy himself refers to the land as *Mantua Ursaria*.

The bear has been a symbol of Madrid since the early 13th century and appears in the city's coat of arms. The blue border with seven white stars represent the seven stars of the Great Bear constellation known in Latin as *Ursa Major*. Others believe that the seven white stars represent the mythical Seven Schools of Astronomy that are believed to have existed in Medina Mayrit during the late 10th century.

Coat of Arms of Madrid

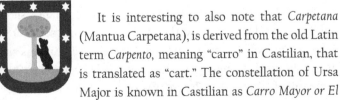

It is interesting to also note that *Carpetana* (Mantua Carpetana), is derived from the old Latin term *Carpento*, meaning "carro" in Castilian, that is translated as "cart." The constellation of Ursa Major is known in Castilian as *Carro Mayor or El*

Carro. You will also find the emblematic Madrone bear and seven stars on the pedestal of an early 19th century fountain on c/ Toledo in Madrid known as *Fuentecilla* or "little fountain." Crowning the fountain that once had the freshest water in the city, is a sculpture of a lion representing the Spanish monarchy.

Fuentecilla

It is said that "all main roads in Spain lead to Madrid." The Puerta del Sol is situated at the exact geographical center or "Km 0" of

Spain. In 1950, a ceramic plaque or flagstone was installed on the pavement just south of the Puerta del Sol. The plaque displays a map of Spain with its six radial national roads, known as *Nacionales I to VI*, leading to the Basque region, Catalonia, Galicia, Valencia, Andalusia, and Extremadura.

KM 0

At the top of the building at the south side at Puerta del Sol known as the emblematic *Real Casa de Correos*, you will see a clock tower that was installed during the 19th century that replaced another from the 18th century. The original purpose of this clock was to remind the Christian citizens of Madrid to say an *Ave Maria* prayer every day at noon. The clock is referred to as *El Reloj de Gobernación* and stands as a meeting place for both locals and visitors alike.

As in Times Square in New York City, thousands gather at Puerta del Sol on New Year's Eve to celebrate the coming year. During the clock's final twelve strokes at midnight every year, 12 grapes are eaten that are believed to bring luck for the New Year. This tradition is dated to 1909 when the grape harvest in Alicante resulted in an enormous surplus, and the harvesters unloaded their grapes by offering them to the citizens on New Year's Eve. The tradition of eating 12 grapes (that represent the months of the coming year) during the last 12 seconds of the old year, while the clock rings the last 12 chimes, means the New Year is ushered in with laughter as mouths are stuffed with grapes.

Reloj de Gobernación, Puerta del Sol

11. *El Viaducto* (The Viaduct) was originally a small bridge mentioned in the Fuero de Madrid of 1202; however, its present form that was inaugurated in 1915 replaced the original construction of 1874. The Muslim wall passed by the northern opening of the Viaduct where the Palace of Malpica once stood. Situated near Cuesta de la Vega, on c/ de Segovia, the Viaduct has often been the location of many suicides as poet Emilio Carrere described:

> *El Viaducto, buen balcón*
> *del soñador nocherniego,*
> *y el trampolín mas seguro*
> *para dar el verdadero*
> *salto mortal, el funámbulo*
> *de lo horrible que en su vuelo*
> *de tragicas volteretas*
> *aterriza en los infiernos.*

Suena un reloj... En la noche
se oyen los pasos del Tiempo.

The Viaduct; fine balcony
of the night dreamer,
and the most dependable trampoline
from which to make
a mortal leap, the acrobat
and his horrible flight
of tragic tumbles
lands in hell.
A clock sounds... In the night
you can hear the passing of time.

Viaduct

12. The largest and most popular open air flea market in the country takes place every Sunday in Madrid. Situated in the working-class district of Lavapiés and La Latina, the flea market known as *El Rastro* is where one can find 3,500 stalls displaying a gigantic variety of new and used products.

The name El Rastro is translated to "the trail" or "the stain" from the Castilian verb arrastrar meaning "to drag" or "to haul." Reason being that during the late 15th century and early 16th century, slaughtered cattle were transported or hauled to the local tanneries nearby leaving a trail of blood behind along these streets. As the blood of these animals flowed down c/ de las Tenerías (Street of the Tanneries), the profession of a tanner survives in the name as it is known today as c/ Ribera de Curtidores (Riverbank of the Tanners Street.) At the end of the 17th century and during the 18th century, tanners began to sell tools and equipment at the market however, since the 19th century, it has been a large flea market every Sunday morning where all that is imaginable is bargained, bought, and sold.

"The Surrender of Breda by Velázquez" by Manuel Ruiz, 1932

13. Madrid has over 70 museums to visit including the *Reina Sofia* and *Thyssen* museums as well as the world-respected *El Prado* Museum. In 1930, when my father was ten years old, he frequently visited the Prado Museum to study the colors used by such great

masters as El Greco (1541–1614), Velázquez (1599–1660), Murillo (1617–1682), Goya (1746–1828), and Sorolla (1863–1923), by reproducing their works. My aunt remembers that crowds would gather to watch her brother sketch at the Prado Museum. Here is the only photograph of one of those paintings by my father when he was a young boy of 12 years old. (*The Surrender of Breda*, aka *The Lances*, by Velázquez)

My father would rush home with great anticipation to mix the colors to see if he could get just the same hue his idols had used. His works earned him an honorable mention in Madrid when he was 14. Just before he retired, this boy was referred to as the "best watercolorist in Canada during the 1970s and 1980s."

My father subsequently married the daughter of a muse who posed for the son of *Joaquin Sorolla*, who was a famous Spanish painter known as the "master of light"; his works are displayed at his *Museo Sorolla*, the only museum in Madrid that is devoted entirely to one artist.

The museum was created by his widow in 1925 and in 1932 was officially inaugurated by his only son, *Joaquín Sorolla García* (1892–1948), who functioned as the museum director. The museum not only contains his father's artwork but also houses objects of Sorolla's private collections that include jewels, ceramics, sculptures, and historical photographs posing with royalty.

García inherited his father's talent and followed in his artistic footsteps. During the 1940s my grandmother Isabel Marin Serrano often posed as a model for the younger Sorolla at this picturesque house where the museum is located. The original sketches are stored in vaults that the curator was kind enough to show me in 2009. The Sorolla Museum is located in what once was the artists' home and studio: a charming house with plush gardens, flowing fountains, and elaborate patios where my mother remembers playing for hours as a child while her mother posed for the younger artist. The design of the front garden of the house was inspired by the magnificent Generalife Gardens of the Alhambra in Granada.

Sorolla Museum

14. Another completely different yet interesting museum in Madrid is also a Spanish restaurant that is part of a chain known as *Museo de Jamón* (Museum of Ham). A large amount of different kinds of cured hams are exhibited here as they hang displayed from the ceiling. Here you can enjoy the famous aged *Jamón Serrano* and select from their excellent choice of Spanish hams, sausages, cheeses, and appetizers known as *tapas*.

The *Museo de Origenes* (Museum of Origins) at Plaza San Andrés, exhibits Madrid's archaeological heritage from prehistory to the 16th century of our era. Until as recent as 2007, the museum was known as *Museo de San Isidro* or *Casa de San Isidro*, named after Madrid's patron saint, as it was here where he lived and died. Legend has it that in this house San Isidro performed one of his most famous miracles. According to tradition, his only son *Illán* fell into a well and San Isidro caused the water to rise high enough for the boy to be rescued. This well, known as "the miracle well," is still preserved inside the house.

Museo Origenes

Museo Jamon

San Isidro Labrador was a farm laborer known best for his kind and charitable heart. He was born in Madrid around 1082 to a humble Mozárabe family and died in 1172. His body along with that of his wife, *Santa Maria de la Cabeza*, lies in the Cathedral of San Isidro on c/ de Toledo.

15. We know that the patron saint of Madrid is San Isidro, but at the other end of the moral spectrum, who is Madrid's most celebrated bandit or *bandolero*?

Luis Candelas Cajigal was born in the barrio of Lavapiés in Madrid in the year 1804. Candelas was a fashionable man who would boldly wear a turquoise blue bolero jacket, a wide red sash over tight blue pants, and a felt hat that covered his brows. It is said that he would go into the night wearing a black cape decorated with Masonic symbols.

But Candelas was an ingenious man who used his special skills for the wrong reasons. It is difficult to separate the facts from legend, but one thing we know for sure - he stole anything his heart desired: fancy clothes, jewellery, horses, mules, furniture from a warehouse, tools, and much more. Candelas assaulted stagecoaches during the 19th century and executed what today are known as home invasions. However, it was his ingenious way of committing his crimes that set him apart from other bandoleers.

A curious story about the adventures of Luis Candelas involving a fancy cape and buns of stale bread demonstrates his ingenuity. One afternoon as Candelas was casually strolling on c/ Mayor, a gorgeous cape displayed in the window of a tailor shop caught his eye. He wanted nothing more than to possess this fine cape but had no financial means to make it a reality. Not to be deterred by this, that same afternoon the cape was his.

Dressed in his best clothes, he puts his newly devised plan into motion: Candelas enters a bakery and makes the most preposterous request. To the astonishment of the shop owner, Candelas orders three dozen *duros* (hard), referring to stale buns. The intrigued owner asks why he wishes these stale buns and Candelas replies that he wants to play a prank on a friend. Realizing that this is a good opportunity to unload his old bread while having a bit of fun at the same time, the baker quickly goes into the back of the store and returns with 36 of his hardest buns.

After some haggling, the men agree on a price and Candelas pays the merchant. Just as he is about to leave, Candelas asks the owner to hold onto the hard buns for a very short while until he returns to the shop with the friend that he is supposedly tricking.

Candelas leaves the premises and heads towards the tailor shop. He approaches the salesman, asking the price of the gorgeous cape — to which he displays an exaggerated response, as it was quite expensive. The banter goes back and forth until Candelas finally agrees on a price. He then dons the cape and asks the salesman to fetch an employee of the store to accompany him, as insurance, to the nearby bakery where he says that the owner owes him the money that he would use to make the purchase.

From the door of the bakery and under the watchful eye of the tailor-shop owner, Luis Candelas says to the baker, "Of those *duros* that you are holding for me, give this guy thirty, and two more as a tip!" The baker complies, enjoying his part in the supposed prank but unaware of what was actually taking place. While the baker goes into his store to retrieve the buns, Candelas disappears, with the cape upon his shoulders. The reader may be somewhat confused at this point. Let me explain that stale buns were not the only thing called *duro* ("hard"); a monetary unit used in Spain during the 19th century was called the same. Luis Candelas acquired the luxurious cape for the price of 36 stale buns.

Candelas continued his misadventures, keeping the citizens of Madrid in both fear and awe during the first half of the 19th century. On the 6th of November in 1837, Luis Candelas was executed by garrotting at Plaza de la Cebada; his lasts words were:

> He sido pecador como hombre, pero nunca se mancharon mis manos con la sangre de mis semejantes. Digo esto porque me oye el que va a recibirme en sus brazos. Adiós Patria mía, sé feliz!

> As a man I have sinned, but my hands were never dirtied by the blood of my fellow men. I say this so that he who will receive me in his arms hears me. Goodbye Motherland, be happy!"

One of the taverns where Luis Candelas and his band of bandits reunited and found shelter after an escapade is located at an establishment at Arco de Cuchilleros at the south-west corner of Playa Mayor. This locale is known as *Las Cuevas de Luis Candelas* (The Caves of Luis Candelas) that once served as an ideal hideout providing a quick and easy getaway with its multiple escape exits. The legend continues as it is said that Candelas hid his stolen treasures in the cellar of this tavern that have never been found. Today, this historical locale is a restaurant specializing in *horno de asar* or roasts in a wood-fired oven and is considered to be one of the finest restaurants in Madrid.

Cuevas Candelas

16. Today, the population of Muslims in Madrid is quite large equipped with its own mosques and Islamic cultural centers throughout the city. The Islamic Cultural Center of Madrid on c/ Salvador de Madariaga is locally known as "La Mezquita" (the Mosque) and was innaugurated in 1992. The building stands as the largest of its kind in the country that was built in honor of the Muslims who founded the city.

This visually stunning white complex houses a mosque, an extensive multi-lingual library, a school for children, a Lebanese restaurant known as *Al Zahra*, as well as a conference room and an exhibition hall. The center offers such activities as sport competitions, sewing courses for women, as well as Arabic language classes. The design of the complex was inspired by the architectural style of the majestic Mosque in Córdoba combined with modern elements. As it stands by the M-30 motorway it is also known as the Mezquita M-30.

Mosque M30 (above) and Mosque Abu Bakr (below)

The second biggest mosque in Madrid is known as the Central Mosque or *Masjid Abu-Bakr* and is situated in the predominantly Muslim district of Tetuán de las Victorias. Inaugurated in 1988, this four-storey building houses not only a mosque but an auditorium, shop, nursery, a school, and a library.

17. A crucial element of the Islamic religion is cleanliness on a daily basis and Arab bath houses filled this purpose. Records exists of baths being situated next to the San Pedro stream (c/ Segovia) and c/ de los Caños (Drain Street) named after the numerous drain pipes that supplied water to the public bath houses.

It is said that all Arab bath houses were destroyed by Alfonso VIII who believed that baths were detrimental as they relaxed and weakened the troops, rendering them useless for battle. Another theory for his ban against the baths could have been the need to preserve water for the more significant task of supplying it to the royal gardens of the Queen's palace.

A modern Arab bath house can be found today in downtown Madrid. The inscription at the door reads that the baths are "situated beneath a century-old water tank." The establishment is known as *Medina Mayrit* and is located on c/ Atocha. Clients can benefit here from steam baths, massages, and aromatherapy, while traditional Arab dishes are served in the restaurant and a selection of teas, shakes, and natural juices to chose from in the *tetería* or tearoom. A belly dance show is featured in the restaurant and in the tearoom during weekend afternoons.

Cibeles

Neptuno

18. Over a dozen fountains dot the picturesque city of Madrid. Along with the fountain of Cibeles, the fountain of Neptune is also visually stunning. Dedicated to the Roman god of the sea, the sculpture is dated to the late 18th century and forms a trio along with the fountains of Cibeles and Apollo.

During the 1940s when food was scarce—it was rationed in Madrid and throughout the country after the civil war—the statue appeared one morning with the following humorous phrase inscribed upon a poster pinned to his trident:

> *Pido con harto dolor,*
> *el que, o me deis de comer*
> *o quitadme el tenedor.*

> *With much pain I ask,*
> *either give me food*
> *or take my fork away.*

The fountain of Neptune is situated close to the Prado Museum and it is here where the *Atletico de Madrid* soccer team celebrates their victories.

19. Spain's number one sport, football, or soccer as it is known in North America, is home to the capital's *Real Madrid* team. Several members of the Real Madrid team helped to win the European Cup for Spain in 2008 and the World Cup in 2010.

20. Flamenco was born in southern Spain, emerging during the late 15th century among the Gypsies of Seville and Cadiz. It is in Andalusia where Flamenco is best preserved, specifically in Seville.

Madrid, however, has a variety of fine venues where this art form can be appreciated. Among several are *Corral de la Morería* on c/ Morería and *Casa Patas* on c/ Cañizares: both known for being the best the capital has to offer in terms of authentic flamenco. (*8.23 Corral de la Morería*)

Only late in 2010, has Flamenco finally been recognized by UNESCO as an Intangible Cultural Heritage of Humanity.

Flamenco

21. Madrid is the capital of bullfighting in Spain. The first spectacle in the villa took place in 1474. The largest bullfight ring in the country is found in Madrid in the form of a neo-Mudéjar building known as *Plaza de Toros Las Ventas*, named after the neighborhood that it is located, *Las Ventas del Espiritu Santo*. Construction began in 1922 and the first bull fight here took place in 1931 when the ring was not fully completed. The bullring that accommodates up to 23,798 spectators is considered to be the most important venue in the world of tauromachy or bullfighting and is often dubbed "The Cathedral of Bullfighting."

Las Ventas (above) and *Matador (below)*

22. The best preserved castle in the province and one of the most important in the country is situated about 30 miles north of Madrid known as *Manzanares el Real* (The Royal Manzanares.) The magnificent structure is also known as *El Castillo de los Mendoza* (The Castle of the Mendozas) and was built over the ruins of a 13th century Mudéjar chapel. The fortress as we see it today was finalized during the late 15th century by Íñigo López de Mendoza. El Manzanares is open to the public and you can also the visit its congress hall, exhibition hall, library, and museum within the complex. The ruins of the old castle that lie nearby are known as the *Plaza de Armas* (Plaza of Weapons.) Little is known of this structure that first appeared documented during the late 14th century.

23. The 16th century *Monasterio de El Escorial* is considered to be one the most beautiful complexes in the province that is situated approximately 30 miles northwest from downtown Madrid. Amidst magnificent landscape in the foothills of the Sierra de Guadarrama, King Felipe II, son of Roman Emperor Carlos V, intended the building complex to serve as a monastery, a palace, and a mausoleum. Felipe II ordered its construction six years after the victory of Spain over the French in the summer of 1557 at the Battle of St. Quentin in France. The king himself rests eternally in the *Panteón de los Reyes* (royal pantheon) that also houses the remains of many kings and queens of Spain as it was also a burial place for the royal family. Curiously, a number of severed heads of saints and a vast assortment of limbs and body parts are actually included in the collection.

The Escorial took 21 years to be built and contains over 300 rooms. Within is a wealth of exquisite tapestries and fine paintings by such artists as El Greco and Velázquez. Within El Escorial you will also find a museum, a school, and library containing classic Latin, Hebrew, Greek, and Arabic manuscripts and books. The library itself is considered to have one of the most significant collections in the world. The Monastery and Site of the Escorial is declared a World Heritage Site by UNESCO.

Spain is the second country after Italy with the most UNESCO sites on the World Heritage List. There are 42 monuments, natural sites and towns honored with this title in the country of which three are in Madrid: in addition to the Escorial, the University and Historic Precinct of Alcalá de Henares as well as the Aranjuez Cultural Landscape are also on the World Heritage List of UNESCO.

24. Within the European Union, Madrid is the third most populated city after London and Berlin. Named European Cultural Capital of 1992, it stands as the largest city in the country with the highest population composed of 21 districts. This multicultural city has a population of over 3 million and has been estimated at receiving 7 million tourists every year. Madrid continues to attract numerous immigrants from around the world, mainly from eastern European countries as well as South America.

Not only is the largest financial center in the country it is also one of the largest in Europe as it functions as a major hub for international commerce and business ventures. Madrid is also known as the fashion capital of the country and the most nocturnal city in Europe. However as most of Madrid, described by James A. Michener in "Iberia: Spanish Travels and Reflections" as a masculine city, was rebuilt during the 20th century, it is therefore considered by some as one of the least typical Spanish cities in the country.

25. Madrid is generally accepted as being the highest capital in the continent at around 2132 feet above sea level. This is reflected in the popular saying among Madrileños:

De Madrid al cielo, y, en el cielo, un agujerito para verlo.

From Madrid to heaven, and from heaven, a little hole to see it through.

This aphorism was quite popular at the end of the 18th century; it suggests the clear blue skies and soft breezes of Madrid are as close to heaven or paradise as one can possibly get.

The Author

9. Etymology

In Medina Mayrit, Arabic was spoken by the Moors and a Latin Romance dialect was spoken by the Mozárabes. After the Reconquest, the remaining Arabs and Berbers began to speak the local Romance dialect and by the 15th century, thousands of Arabic words had integrated into the language. Although Spanish or Castilian, the official language of Spain, is derived from Latin, it is Arabic that follows as contributing the most to the language.

Few cities were actually founded in al-Andalus by the Moors as most were built over Phoenician, Greek, Roman, or Visigoth settlements. The Moors generally maintained the original Latin names of the many towns they occupied; however, they adapted or modified them to their language. Examples can be heard in the Andalusian provinces of Seville that was known as *Ishbillya* by the Moors adapted from the Roman *Hispalis* and Phoenician *Sephela*: Málaga, that was pronounced as *Malakah* by the Moors and Romans, is derived from its Phoenician name of *Malaq Qart*, meaning "Royal City", and Córdoba, known as *Qurtuba* by the Moors, is derived from the Phoenician *Qart Tuba* or "City of Tuba," referring to the Semitic deity also known as *Ba'al*. Therefore, many names of cities in Spain have origins going back much further than the Moors as they simply adapted, or distorted if you will, the original name. However, cities such as Madrid that were originally founded by the Moors retain a modified version of their Arabic name as do Calatrava and Catalifa that we shall soon explore.

Just about every word, city or town in Spain that begins with "al" is also of Arabic origin; *al* is the Arabic prefix equivalent to "the." Two examples include *Albacete*, derived from *al-basit*, meaning "the plain", is composed of flat terrain and *Alcántara*, derived from *al-qantara* translated as "the bridge", as this town in Cáceres took its name from the local Roman bridge that is widely considered an architectural masterpiece.

The term *al-Andalus* itself has several etymological theories attached to it. The name first appeared inscribed upon a gold dinar dated to 716 that is presently on display at the Archaeological Museum of Madrid. The coin displays the Latin inscription *Span* (Spania) on one side and in Arabic script *al Andalus* on the reverse. A common theory is that *al-Andalus* is derived from *Vandalusia*, translated as "Land of the Vandals." However, this seems unlikely as these Germanic tribes exerted little influence in the region during their brief, uneventful reign that lasted from 409 to 429 ADE.

The most accepted theory is that the origins lie in the Arabic pronunciation of the name used by the Visigoths for the region, *Landa-hlauts*. In old German, this term means "land of allotments", as it was the Germanic custom and tradition to divide and distribute their conquered lands amongst themselves through a raffle or what we would today call a lottery.

It stands to reason that when the Moors first arrived in southern Spain, they most likely pronounced it as *Landalos* and naturally added their prefix of *al*, resulting in *al-Andalus*. Various etymological theories are attributed to the Visigoths and their East Germanic language. As these tribes became romanized their language eventually consisted of a Latin dialect with Germanic influences. Many of these words handed down from the Spanish Visigoths are related to warfare and military. Although few in number, some examples include *guerra* or "war" derived from *werra; pistola* or "pistol" derived from *pistole;* and *guardia* or "guard" derived from *wardaz.*

However, not all Castilian terms and place names that are of Arabic origin exclusively begin with *al*. Two such examples lie in the names of the towns of *Medinaceli* in Soria, derived from *Madinat Salim* (named after the Berber tribe of *Banu Salim*) and *Benicasim* in Castellón, derived from the *Banu Qasim* (named after the Basque-Muladí tribe of *Banu-Qasi*).

Additional Arabisms are found in the fields of architecture, astronomy, and botany. The Moors also introduced numerous types of flowers, plants, and scents to al-Andalus such as *almizcle* or "musk" from *al-misk* and *azucena* or "white lily" from *as-susana*. We find even more Arabisms in the fields of business and commerce for example: *zoco* meaning "market," derived from *suq*, as well as *almacén* meaning "storehouse" deriving from *al-mahzan*. Many irrigation devices are known today by their Arabic name in Castilian form:

aceña or "water mill" derived from *as-saniya* or "the lifter"

acequia or "irrigation channel" derived from *as-saqiya* or "the canal"

aljibe or "cistern" derived from *al-jubb* or "the reservoir"

alcantarilla or "sewer/drain" derived from *al-qantarah* or "the (little) bridge."

almenara or "canal" derived from *al-manahir*.

noria or "hydraulic wheel", derived from *an-na'wra* or "the water wheel."

Arabisms are also found in the literature, mathematics, medicine, poetry, and music of Spain; even the expression of *olé* is derived from the Arabic *wa' Allah* meaning "praise Allah." More words of Arabic origin can also be found in Spanish cuisine as the Moors introduced many essential foods and spices into the peninsula long ago such as *azafrán* or "saffron" derived from *az-zafaran* and *albahaca* or "basil" derived from *al-habaqah*. Fruits such as *albaricoque* or "apricots" derived from *al-barquq*; *limón* or "lemon" derived from *al-laymun*; and *naranja* or "orange" derived from *an-naranj*, all retain a version of their Arabic name. Also introduced by the Moors was *arroz* or "rice" derived from *ar-ruzz*; *azúcar* or "sugar" derived from *as-sukkar*; and *aceite* or "oil" from *az-zayt*.

Although many of the terms explored here are of Arabic and Latin origin, there are others that in addition to German that are also derived from the Basque or *Euskera*, Celtiberian, Greek, and Hebrew languages. The following is a glossary of Castilian place-names and terms that have appeared throughout the chapters along with their etymological theories, with the proper Castilian pronunciation when it considerably varies from that of English.

Adarve (A-DARveh): This term is derived from the Arabic *ad-darb* meaning "the alley." The adarve was the narrow passageway located inside a gate on the main street that was either behind or above a wall that led to private houses.

Ajedrez (Ahe-DRETH): The game of chess was known by the Moors as *ash-shatranj*, derived from the Persian *shatranj* that in turn is derived from the Sanskrit *Chaturanga*, named after the four divisions of the Indian army. Ajedrez or chess is believed to have been introduced during the 9th century by a man named *Ziryab* who also brought the game of polo to al-Andalus. Ziryab, of Kurdish origin, traveled from Persia to Córdoba to explore his multitude of creative ideas. The capital of Córdoba, during the 9th and 10th centuries, was experiencing its Golden Age and it was at this time when it flourished as an Islamic center as the most powerful and richest state in Western Europe.

Ziryab, or *Abd-al Hasan Ali-ibn Nafi*, was a man of many talents, an innovative genius, and a trendsetter. He was an expert in such fields of medicine, astronomy, astrology, geography, and philosophy, but above all he was renowned musician, poet, composer, and singer. Ziryab came to Córdoba to serve within the court as chief musician to the father of the founder of Medina Mayrit, Abd ar-Rahman II.

He is also credited with setting fashion trends and hairstyles, opening a school of music, introducing the lute or *oud*, as well as bringing Persian and Hindu musical styles to southern Spain that are still heard today in Andalusí music.

Alamillo (Ala-MEE-yo): In the area of the old Morería of Madrid stands the plaza and street of Alamillo. This term may be derived from the Arabic alamín who is the supreme authority of the mosque. It was here where he resided and held town council as well as court meetings. However, others believe that the plaza and street is named after the poplar tree or álamo that once stood in the center of the plaza that was destroyed by a hurricane during the 16th century. Nineteenth century author Antonio Hurtado Valhondo who died in Madrid in 1878 pays tribute:

En la antigua Morería,
barrio en Madrid conocido,
hay una calle llamada
la calle de Alamillo.

Tuvo origen este nombre,
hará cosa de tres siglos,
en un árbol medio enteco
que, a la ventura nacido,
en el confín de la calle
brillaba ufano y altivo,
con presunciones de grande
y realidades de chico.

Columpio eterno del aire,
columpio eterno de nidos,
murmurador de gorjeos
y fingidor de suspirios,
era el alamo el encanto...

In the old Morería,
well-known quarter of Madrid,
is a street named
the street of Alamillo.

Having the origin of this name,
about three centuries ago
in a tree somewhat feeble
that, as fortune would have it was born,

in the confines of the street
shining proud and tall,
with presumptions of grandeur
and modest realities.

Eternal swing of air,
eternal swing of nests,
whisperer of trills
and mimicker of sighs,
was the enchanted álamo.....

Alarife (Ala-RIFeh): An Alarife is a type of specialized architect and master in brick-work. The term is derived from *ar-arif* meaning "the expert" or "the knowledgeable one" in Arabic. The Mudéjars were known as being quite skilled in this profession that was regarded as a most prestigious occupation.

The impressive summer palace and recreational gardens by the Alhambra of Granada is known as *Generalife* and pronounced as "henera-lee-feh." Its name is derived from the Arabic *Ganna al-Arif* that translates as "Garden of the Architect." The palace and gardens were created to reflect paradise on earth as the Muslims regarded Allah as "the architect of the universe."

Alcalá de Henares (Alca-LA de ENAres): About 20 miles from Madrid, Alcalá de Henares was known by the Romans as *Complutum* during the 1st century BCE. Several theories are proposed for its etymology; some state that it is derived from its Greek name of the town of *Komeploutus*, composed of *kome* meaning "village" and *ploutus* meaning "wealth" or "riches." Another theory is of Latin origins as it may derive from *compluvium*, meaning "place where rivers converge." Others subscribe to the etymology as being Pre-Roman as a coin dated to Celtiberian occupation was discovered in the area bearing the name of *Ikesancom Komboutu*.

The Moors interestingly completely renamed the village *Qal'at Abd es-Salam* translated to "Castle of the Servant of Peace" or simply "Castle of Salim", after a member of the prominent Berber family known as Banu Salim. However, Muhammad I renamed the settlement as *Qal'at an-Nahar* translated as "Castle on the River."

During the beginning of the 16th century, the *Universidad Complutense* was founded in Alcalá de Henares by Cardinal Cisneros that was the first of its kind. Here, theology, medicine, and law were studied and it soon became a leading intellectual center. Alcalá de Henares is also the birthplace of the 16th century novelist Miguel de Cervantes (1547–1616) who died in Madrid. Cervantes is the esteemed author of "Don Quijote de la Mancha" that is considered to be one of the finest works of literature ever published.

Alcazába (Alka-THAba): A small city, usually of a military character found within another larger walled city, is known as an Alcazába. Of a defensive structure, the Alcazába catered to the military population of the city. The term is derived from the Arabic *al-qasbah* meaning "the citadel" or "the fortified area."

Alcázar (Al-KAthar): The castle or royal palace of a Moorish town is known as an Alcázar. Adhering to Muslim tradition, it consisted of a defensive structure constructed high upon a hill within the city's wall that often served as refuge for the population when attacked by enemies. The term is derived from the Arabic *al-qasr* with a similar meaning as *al-qalat*.

Alcázars, throughout al-Andalus, were fortified and rebuilt by the conquering Christians. They served as residences or castles for royalty and were ornamented with decorative fountains, picturesque courtyards, and lavish gardens. The first reference to the Alcázar of Madrid is dated to the mid 14th century.

Aljamia (Alha-MEEya): The systematic form of writing in the Romance language that developed in al-Andalus that was written in Arabic or Hebrew script is known as Aljamia. This term derives from the Arabic *aj-jamiyya* that translates as "foreign" or "non-Arabic."

The use of Arabic, whether spoken or written, was prohibited in Spain during the late 15th century and Aljamia, with origins in the Mozárabe language, was therefore created and spoken by the Moriscos. This language was used in daily communications as well as in the recording and preserving of Islamic religious beliefs, prayers, and traditions. Manuscripts transcribed from the Mozárabic or *Ladino* (spoken by Spanish Jews) languages written in the Arabic alphabet are known as being *Aljamiado*. During the 9th and 10th century, poetry, song, and literature written in Aljamia were quite popular such as the *Muwashahas, Jarchas*, and *Zejels* that were introduced by Ziryab. The following table illustrates the influence of the Arabic language from texts written in Mozárabic or Aljamiado with their correspondin

English	Castilian	Arabic	Mozárabic
White	Blanco	Abyad	Albo
Red	Rojo	Hamra	Hamrella
Blonde	Rubia	Shaqra	Saqrella
Time	Tiempo	Zaman	Zameni
Before	Antes	Qabl	Qabl
Sir/Lord	Señor	Sayyid	Cid
Mercy	Clemencia	Rahima	Rahima
Two Eyes	Dos Ojos	Aynayn	Aynayn
My love	Mi amor	Habibi	Habib
Truth	Verdad	Haqq	Haqq
Separate	Separar	Firaq	Firaq

Almagil (Alma-JEEL): The common Castilian word for "mosque" is *mezquita* but it is also known as an "almagil"; that is derived from the Arabic *al-masjid* meaning "the mosque." The two principal mosques in Madrid today are the Main Mosque or Islamic Cultural Center of Madrid in the Ventas neighborhood and the Central Mosque or *Abu-Bakr Mosque* in the Tetuan district.

Alminar: The tower of a mosque is known as an "alminar" that is derived from the Arabic *al-minar* meaning the same. The tower on the church of San Nicolás in old Madrid is believed to have originally functioned as an "alminar."

Almudena: Derived from the Arabic *al-mudayna* that translates as "the little city" or "citadel", the Almudena was a fortified or urban nucleus situated within a walled surrounding. Along with Madrid's cathedral, the patron saint, la Virgen de Almudena, was given this title as her image was found hidden near the citadel during the 11th century. Yet others however, subscribe to the theory that she is so named because her image was discovered near an *almudin* or wheat storehouse.

Cathedral

Seventeenth century Spanish writer *Diego Juan de Vera Tassis y Villarroel* proposed a debatable etymology for "almudena" as follows: *al* (from *alma* "virgin" in Hebrew), and from Latin *mu* (from mulier or "mother"), *de* (from *dei* or "God"), *na* (from *natus* or "birth"). This he translates as "Virgin mother who gave birth to God." However, we might reasonably speculate that the "alma" also came from Latin, where it means "nourishing", thus giving us "Nourishing mother who gave birth to God" (or "Nourishing mother goddess by birth)."

Alquerque (Al-KERkeh): The popular game of checkers introduced to al-Andalus by the Moors, was known as *al-qirkat* or *al-qirq* in Arabic that roughly translates as "the playing area." Al-Qirkat, with goots going back to ancient Egypt, is mentioned in the 9th century work *Kitab al-Aghani* (The Book of Songs), by the 13th century, it appears in Spanish manuscripts as Alquerque.

Andújar (An-DOOhar): In the Andalusian province of Jaén, Andujar is situated upon a hill above the Guadalquivir River. The origin of its name goes back to the Celtiberians who named the region *Andura* that translates as "abundance of water" named so because of its proximity to the Guadalquivir and the many streams and rivers in the area. This name persisted in Roman Spain and during Moorish rule it was pronounced as *Andusar* until the 13th century when it was conquered by the Christians and evolved into its present form. The first mention we have of this town goes back to the year 854 corresponding to the reign of Muhammad I when the Toledans rebelled and ambushed the Moors in Andújar.

Aragón: The autonomous community of Aragón found in the northeast of Spain is composed of the provinces Huesca, Teruel, and its capital of Zaragoza. Of the many theories that surround the etymology of the name, the most sound appears to be of Basque origin. The term *haran* meaning valley and *goi* meaning "high" or "tall." Aragón has always played a most significant role in the history and unification of Christian Spain.

Aranjuez (Aran-HUETH): Located about 30 miles southeast of Madrid on the Tagus River, Aranjuez was once a summer retreat for royalty. Its etymology may consist of the Arabic term *arankej* meaning "place of many walnuts." Another theory is that it is derived from the Latin *Ara Jovis* meaning "Altar of Jove"; Jove being Jupiter, the Roman king of gods.

However, the most popular theory is that its origins are Basque; *Aranz* was the ancient name for the village and in the Basque language it means "Land of Hawthorns." The hawthorn, a type of small tree or shrub, is known as *arantza* in Basque. It is worth emphasizing at this point that the Basque language resembles no other known to man and as a result, its origins remain unknown.

Arganda del Rey: Prehistoric deposits and archaeological ruins dating to the Roman Era have been discovered in this municipality of Madrid. The name of this town may be derived from its Celtiberian name of *Uriaganda* meaning "Land of the Waters." Some believe that its origins lie in the Celtiberian prefix of *ar* that signifies "extreme" or "away from" and *ganda* meaning "hard" or "high" or "rocky", referring to the land. Others agree that it its etymology is Celtiberian however, is derived from *arkanta* meaning "silver." Another theory is that it is attributed to being Latin in origin deriving from the terms *area* and *canda* meaning "white area" or "bright area".

The addition of "del Rey", translating as "of the King", refers to King Felipe II who during the late 16th century, purchased the town for 10,000 ducats. Today, Arganda del Rey is easily connected to Madrid by underground metro or subway.

Arrabal: The populated area outside a walled Muslim city is known as an *arrabal*, derived from the Arabic *ar-rabad* meaning "the suburb." Today's central Plaza Mayor, built during the early 15th century, was once the traditional Muslim market area known as *La Plaza del Arrabal*. The term *arrabal* is still in use in Castilian today; however, it denotes a working class suburb or neighborhood.

Many arrabales arose in Madrid between the 12th and 16th centuries due to the increase in population and expansion of the city. One such important arrabal was San Martín that was founded by Alfonso VII in 1126. This suburb, that reached a population of 18,000 inhabitants, was situated where Plaza de San Martín and Plaza de las Descalzas are today.

Another important arrabal was Santa Cruz dated to the 13th century that did not reach its peak until the first half of the 15th century. This neighborhood was situated south of arrabal San Martín.

The arrabal of San Ginés was located between Puerta de Guadalajara and Puerta del Sol; between San Martin and Santa Cruz. The oldest reference to this arrabal is dated to the mid 14th century.

Near the Puerta del Sol you will find the Iglesia de San Ginés that was originally constructed during the 12th or 13th century. The church that we see today is a complete reconstruction dated to 1645 as the original structure was destroyed three years earlier. Initially, the building was designed in Mudéjar style; however all that remains today is the campanile or bell tower from that era. The church of San Ginés houses artwork by such renowned artists as El Greco (1541–1614) and Alonso Cano (1601–1667.)

San Gines

Another notable arrabal was San Millán that was situated south of Puerta Cerrada and existed at least since the mid 15th century.

This was the last of the arrabales in Madrid to arise during this time period.

Asturias. In this province were the mountainous regions that the Moors were not able to conquer and as a result, it became the first Christian territory to arise after the defeat of the Visigoths in the Iberian Peninsula. Its etymology is believed to be derived from the Basque words *aitza* (rock) and *ura* (water.) It may also be related or derived from the name of the small town of *Astorga* in the province of León.

Astorga was founded as *Astúrica Augusta* by the Romans in 14 BCE. Pliny regarded it as a magnificent city and important administrative military town that was located at the intersection of four important roads. Impressive ruins of Roman baths dated to the 1st century can be visited here. During the Muslim Era, the town's name was pronounced as *Ashtorkah*.

Asturias

Atalaya: An Islamic circular watchtower that was set high upon a hill for the purpose of military vigilance is known as an *atalaya*. During times of impending invasions, signals were sent from a network of these towers when danger approached. The term is derived from the Arabic *at-tala'ia*, meaning "the sentinels" or "the watchtowers." In Castillian, the verb *atalayar* is also used to signify "observe", "watch" or "spy."

In Medina Mayrit the atalayas were constructed during the reigns of Muhammad I and Abd ar-Rahman III. The best preserved Muslim watchtower, known as *Torrelodones*, is located about 20 miles from the city, while the ruins of another nearby is named *Torrecilla* Vestiges of watchtowers that have been discovered in the area are on display the Archaeological Museum of Madrid.

Ávila: Situated about 70 miles north-west of Madrid, Ávila is best known for its highly impressive old town walls dated to the late 11th and early 12th centuries. These structures are comprised of 88 watchtowers and nine gates that are considered to be the best preserved of its kind in the continent.

Ávila is believed to have been founded by the Celtiberian tribe of the *Vettones* during the 5th century BCE as *Obila* that translates as "high mountain." As a stronghold of the Visigoth Kingdom, Ávila became part of the Taifa Kingdom of Toledo during the 11th century when it was known as *Abila*. In 1985, Ávila was named a World Heritage Site by UNESCO.

Avila

Barajas (Ba-RAhass): The international airport of Madrid, located about 9 miles from downtown Madrid is named after the municipality of its location of *Barajas*. The term may be derived from the Hebrew *beraja* meaning "blessing" or from the Arabic *barakah* meaning "luck" that has a similar meaning.

During the Roman Era, Barajas may have been known as *Varada*. Roman vestiges have been excavated here in the form of ceramic oven parts, household goods, bronze vessels, iron tools, and remnants of their opulent villas.

In Castilian, the word *barajas* is also used to refer to a deck of playing cards. The Spanish deck, which originated from the Tarot of ancient Egypt, was quite popular in Spain specifically during the 14ᵗʰ to 16ᵗʰ centuries. Today you can find older locals playing cards in bars or even in groups of families playing on the beaches, as it remains a popular pastime for Spaniards.

By c/ Mayor and c/ de Segovia you will find the charming Plaza of the *Conde de Barajas* named after the Count of Barajas, a steward of the king who lived during the 16ᵗʰ century. A section of the Christian wall was discovered where his palace once stood.

Barcelona (Bartheh-lona): Located about 310 miles from Madrid, Barcelona was known as *Barkeno* by the Phoenicians. According to legend, it was founded by Hercules around 7 BCE and rebuilt by Carthaginian General *Hamilcar Barca* around 250 BCE who named it *Barcino* after himself. When the Visigoths arrived around 400 ADE, they renamed it *Barcinona* that the Moors later pronounced *Barshelonah*.

After Madrid, Barcelona is the second largest city in the country. It is the capital of *Cataluña* (Catalonia) a name that may be derived from *Gothalania*, a term merging the names of the *Goths* and *Alans* tribes who invaded Eastern Spain after the fall of the Romans during the early 5ᵗʰ century.

Ptolemy mentions in his *Geography* among several, a Celtic tribe named *Catalauni* whose capital was the Gallo-Roman *Catalaunum* occupying today the region in France known as Châlons-sur-Marne. This area became an important historical site centuries later as it was here where the Roman victory over the Visigoths took place in 451 ADE at the Battle of Châlons. Catalonia borders France and as a result the Catalan language bears some resemblance to French.

Andalusi-Muslim historian and geographer *Al 'Udri* (1003–1085) mentions a place named *Taluna* or *Taluniya* during Arab rule in the region of Barcelona and Girona. It may have been known during Muslim rule as *Qal'at at-Taluna* meaning "castle of Taluna". Although we have seen this toponym in Alcalá de Henares (*Qal'at an-Nahar*), we find it in several examples of place-names throughout the country including Calatañazor (in Soria) derived from *Qal'at an-Nazor* and the Alhambra (in Granada) derived from *Qal'at al-Hamra*, meaning "red castle."

Alhambra

Yet another etymological theory states that *Cataluña* is derived from the name of a legendary hero from the region named *Otger Catalo* who resisted the Muslims during the mid 8th century.

Bisagra: The name of the gate that looked out into the farmlands of Toledo is known as *Bisagra* derived from the Arabic *bab-xagra* meaning "door to the plains" or "gate of the farmlands." In the Castilian language, the word *bisagra* is also used for a "hinge."

Cáceres (KA-thehrez): Situated 156 miles from Madrid, the historic quarter of Cáceres was named a World Heritage Site by

UNESCO in 1986. The origin of this name may come from the Latin *Castris* or *Castri*, meaning "encampment", as it was here where a Roman military camp was set up during the conquest of Lusitania during the 2nd century BCE. However, in Roman Spain, this town was known as *Norba Caesarina* in memory of Julius Caesar and *Norba* after the Roman general who founded this town.

Calatayud: Located in the province of Zaragoza, Calatayud was fortified by Muhammad I to better handle the rebellions from the Banu Qasi. Its name is derived from the Arabic *Qal'at al-Ayyub* translated as "castle of Ayyub." The fortress was founded in the year 716 by Governor *Ayyub ibn Habib al-Lajmi*, nephew of Musa ibn-Nusayr. Today, you can visit the well preserved wall and towers that were part of a series of defense systems during the Muslim Era existing as one of the oldest of its kind in the country.

Calatrava: Located by the *Guadiana River* in the province of Ciudad Real, Calatrava was known by the Moors as *Qal'at ar-Rabah* meaning "castle of Rabah." It is believed to have been named after the 8th century Abbasid governor *Musa ibn Ollai ibn Rabah*. Another version has it that the name is derived from *Qal'at at-Turab*, meaning "castle of the land."

As the main road that linked Toledo with Córdoba passed through Calatrava, it became a significant strategic point. Before Muhammad I founded Mayrit, he reconstructed a fortress here in Calatrava during 855/856 that was destroyed by the Toledans in their battles against the Umayyads of Córdoba.

During the early 13th century, "la Vieja" was added to the name and it became *Calatrava la Vieja* to differentiate it from *Calatrava la Nueva* (New Calatrava) situated 37 miles further south. Today you can appreciate the ruins of the Alcázar in both the old and new Calatrava.

Carabanchel: This southern suburb of Madrid was first referred to as *Caravanchel* during the late 12th century. It is the location of the significant archaeological discovery of Roman villas. Its etymology may derive from the Persian term *karwan* referring to desert travelers as many commercial caravans that traveled through here. Another theory is that it is derived from the Hebrew *carvan* meaning "anguish" and *chel* meaning "our", as cemeteries were situated here.

Carpetania: This region, where the Celtiberian Carpetanos settled, may have its name origin in the Greek and Latin languages. *Karpos* is the Greek term for "fruit" and *tania* is the Latin term for "land," as an abundance of fruit existed in the area. We see this Latin term in such examples as "Mauritania" (Land of the Berber *Mauri* tribe or land of the Moors), "Lusitania" (land of of the Celtic *Lusus* tribe) and "Brittania" (land of the Celtic *Briton* tribe).

Castilla (Cas-TEEya): This geographical region in the center of Spain was formerly known as the independant Kingdom of Castile or "Castilla" from the 9th to the 15th centuries. Its etymology consists of the Latin *castellum* meaning "castle" (*castillo* in Spanish), for their abundance in the area. The Spanish language is known as *Castellano* (Castilian) and is considered the purest language in the country. It was during the 13th century reign of King Alfonso when historical documents were translated into this dialect becoming the official language of the country.

Catalifa: Along with Talamanca de Jarama and Alcalá de Henares, Catalifa was another of the smaller rural settlements that arose near Medina Mayrit that was cited by Ibn Hayyan in 939. Its etymology consists of the Arabic *Qal'at Jalifah*, meaning "fortress of the Caliph." However, by the middle of the 15th century, the town appears cited as "Odón" and by the early 18th century it is documented as Villaviciosa de Odón. Today you will find the ruins of a well-preserved 15th century castle here that presently houses the Museum of the Spanish Air Force. This town is also home to one of the three campuses of the *Universidad Europea de Madrid*.

Coimbra: Situated in the center of Portugal, Coimbra is home to one of the best preserved Roman archaeological findings of the Iberian Peninsula. The etymology of its name is Celtiberian as it was originally a Celtic settlement. In the Celtiberian language, *conim* refers to a plateau or rocky outcrop and the suffix *-brik* denotes an elevated fortress, defended site, or city. This particular suffix was romanized into *briga*, and the town was known by the Romans as *Conimbriga*. When the Moors arrived in the early 8th century, they pronounced it as *Qulumriyah*.

Covandonga: Situated in Asturias, Covandonga is also the name of the battle where Don Pelayo defeated the Moors in 722. A commanding statue of Pelayo with sword in hand and a Christian cross behind him stands proudly by the Basilica of Covadonga. Its etymology is believed to be Latin as Covandonga was known as *Cova-domna* that translates as "Cave of our Lady."

Cuenca (Kwenka): Located about 75 miles east of Madrid, Cuenca was known as *Conca* during Roman Spain. Its etymology consists of the Latin term *con´chae* for a conch shell. However prior to this, it was known as *Contrebia Cárbica* by the Celtiberians. It is quite possible that the Roman name of *Conca*, is an abbreviated form of *Contrebia* and *Carbica*.

Yet another theory is that *Cuenca* may have been named after the bloodthirsty Spanish-Celtic tribe of the *Concani* and their capital city of *Concana*. It is said that this tribe drank the blood of horses mixed with milk for nourishment. Ptolemy, however, refers to this tribe as settling by the Cantabrian Sea and not in the proximity to present-day Cuenca.

Cuenca was known to the Moors as *Medina Quwinka*, and its Alcázar that was raised in 784 was referred to *Qal'at Qunka*. Al-Idrisi states that Cuenca was a "station" along the way between Córdoba and Zaragoza.

Cuenca was declared a World Heritage Site by UNESCO in 1996 and rightfully so, as the old part of the town is breathtaking. Here you will find the famous *Casas Colgadas* or Hanging Houses that literally hang on the edge of a cliff. These buildings are the most popular attraction of the province. Of these emblematic dwellings, three remain of the many that existed in Cuenca centuries ago. The main and most photographed house is dated to the 15th century and currently houses a museum.

Cuenca

Ebro: The Ebro River rises in the Cantabrian Mountains in the north to the Mediterranean Sea between Barcelona and Valencia to the south-east. It is the most voluminous river with the greatest discharge being the largest and most important in the country. The etymology of the name is possibly Greek or Roman, as they named it *Iber*. However, the origins are most likely Basque as fittingly, the Basque word for "river" is *ibai* and "valley" is *ibar*. It is from here that the term "Iberia" is derived.

Elche (EL-cheh): Situated in the Valencian community of the province of Alicante, Elche was known as *Helike* by the Iberian tribes and as *Illici Augusta* by the Romans. The Visigoths pronounced it as *Elece* and during the 8th century the Moors knew it as *Elsh*.

Today, Elche is a popular beach resort town and is most famous for the discovery of an Iberian sculpture dated to the 5th or 4th century BCE. The sculpture, affectionately known as the "Dama de Elche", is currently on display at the Archaeological Museum of Madrid. Elche has its own archaeological museum that is housed in the 12th century *Palacio de Altamira* that was rebuilt during the 15th century. This town is known as the "palm tree capital of Europe" as it boasts over 200, 000. Impressive Moorish baths can also be visited in Elche dated to the 12th century.

Elche

Less than 10 miles from Elche is the quaint beach town of *Santa Pola*, where the author spent many summer vacations as a child. Here you can appreciate Roman ruins dated to the 5th or 4th century BCE in the form of a restored luxurious villa known as la *Casa Romana del Palmeral* (Palmeral Roman Villa) with its stunning polychrome mosaics of geometrical patterns and decorative painted murals.

Santa Pola

(El) Escorial: The monumental complex and historic royal residence of El Escorial houses a monastery, school, museum, and a royal burial site. Built during the 16th century, it is considered to be the province's finest landmark. The name of the complex may be derived from the term, *escorias*, or "dross," as waste from old iron mines could have been disposed of at this location. However, no evidence exists of such mines in the area, so it may derive from *Aesculus*, a type of oak tree that grew in the vicinity. The least likely theory is that it is derived from the Castilian term *oscuridad*, meaning "darkness", as it is situated amidst a dark, forested, and shadowy landscape. El Escorial, located just outside the city, was declared a UNESCO World Heritage Site in 1984.

Galicia (Ga-LEEtheeya): Located on the northwestern coast of Spain, Galicia was known as *Gallaecia* by the Romans that was later pronounced by the Muslims as *Jalikiyyah*. Its etymology goes back to the name of a Celtic tribe known as the *Callaeci* that settled in the area. The Callaeci worshipped the nature goddess *Cailleach* and named their territory in her honor.

Just below Galicia lies Portugal and there are two theories on the etymology of this country's name. It may be derived from the Latin *portus cale* meaning "warm harbor" or from the Celtic equivalent translated as "port of the Callaecians." In Euskera or the Basque language, the word for street is *Kalea* and in the pictureque Basque harbor village of *Plentzia* there is a street named "Portus Kalea."

Getafe (He-TAfeh): During the early 14th century, this suburb in southern Madrid was known as *Xatafi*. This Arabic term is derived from *xata* meaning something "long", likely referring to the extensive road between Madrid and Toledo where this town is situated. Ruins and artifacts from Roman villas have also been discovered in Getafe.

Guadacelete (Wadatheh-LEHteh): In 854, Muhammad I defeated the Toledans in the battle named after this small river in Toledo.

Its etymology consists of the Arabic *wadj as-Salit* meaning "river of Selit", named after the ancient Yemeni tribe of the *Banu Selit*.

Guadalajara (Wada-lahara): Located approximately 40 miles northeast of Madrid on the Henares River, Guadalajara was founded by the Moors during the 8ᵗʰ century. They named it *Wadj-al-Hadjarat* that translates as "river of stones" or "river that flowed between stones." Although the Arabic term *wadj* refers to a river or valley, in the Andalusian dialect it simply signified "river."

Guadalete (Wada-Lehteh): In the summer of 711, Rodrigo, the last king of Visigoth Spain, lost his life in the battle named after this small river in the southern region of Andalusia that flows from Málaga to Cádiz. *Guadalete* is derived from the Arabic *wadj al-lakka* that translates as "small river".

Guadamur (Wada-MOOR): During the mid 19ᵗʰ century, the spectacular Visigoth votive crowns and gold leaf crosses known as the Guarrazar Treasures were discovered in this municipality of Toledo. *Guadamur* is derived from the Arabic *Wadj al-mur* that translates as "river of the waves." In Guadamur you will find a spectacular 15ᵗʰ century castle somewhat reminiscent of the Alcázar of Segovia.

Guadarrama: Not only is this the name of a town in the community of Madrid, but it is also a mountain range and river in the center of the peninsula. Prior to the 16ᵗʰ century, the somewhat dry Manzanares River was known as the Guadarrama River. Its etymology is Arabic deriving from *Wadj-ar-ramal* meaning "river of sand "or "sandy river."

Guadiana: Both Spain and Portugal share the Guadiana River that flows by the ruins of *Qal'at at Rabah* (Calatrava la Vieja). Its etymology consists of the Arabic *Wadj Ana* or "river of Ana." The term "ana" is borrowed from the town's Latin name of *Flumen Anae* that translates as "old river" as it was known during Roman Spain.

Guarrazar (Wara-THAR): The Visigoth riches discovered in Guadamur, Toledo are known as the Guarrazar Treasures. The etymology of the name is derived from the Arabic *Wadj az-Zahr* or "river of the flower" referring to the orchard where the treasure was accidentally discovered during the 19th century.

Huesca (WESka): Situated in the northern province of Aragón, Huesca was known as *Bolksan* during pre-Roman times. The Romans colonized the area and renamed it *Osca*. That is believed to be derived from Euscs, meaning "Basques," as these people inhabited this region. Another theory is that the Roman name is derived from *Oscians*, a Celtiberian tribe that settled in the area. In al-Andalus, the Moors pronounced it as *Wasqah*.

Jarama (Ha-RAma): In central Spain you will find the Jarama Valley and the largest river of this region that flows through the provinces of Madrid and Guadalajara. The etymology is Arabic deriving from *al-haram* meaning "the sanctuary" or "the sacred place."

Lavapiés (Lava-PEE-es): After the Reconquest, the Jewish population of Madrid is believed to have settled in the area known as Lavapiés; although recently, this theory has come into question. The English translation of this name is "(place of) feet washing", referring to a fountain that once stood in the plaza that was used as a daily absolution or purification ritual by devotees who washed their feet before entering the synagogue. Still others maintain that it was the Christians and Arabs who had to purify their feet before entering and leaving this Jewish neighborhood or Judería. Lavapiés is first mentioned in documents dated to the 16th century in reference to a barter involving the fountain. Two centuries later, the area was known as El Avapiés, but by 19th century it returned to its original and somewhat undignified present name.

Another related theory of the origin of the name *Lavapiés* states that descending streams that flowed in the area bathed or watered the base of the tree groves; hence the watering of the "base" or "feet" of the trees. Today, Lavapiés has a delightful bohemian character as a working class and multicultural suburb filled with bars and ethnic restaurants.

Lavapiés

León: Situated in the northwest of Spain, this town was founded as *Legio* by the Romans during the 1st century BCE, named after the Roman Legion of *Legio VI Victrix*. It was here where Christian King Ramiro II was born. When the Moors arrived they pronounced it as *Liyun*.

Madrid (MaDREETH): The name of Madrid is derived from the Arabic *Mayrit* (pronounced "Majerit", as the "y" in Arabic is pronounced as "dj"), which was its name during its entire Muslim period. The Roman name of *Matrice* (pronounced *Matrich*) persisted not only during Visigoth rule but also throughout Moorish rule as well, and that of their descendants, the Mozárabes. Both these names often competed with each other even after the Reconquest however; it was "Matrice" that succeeded. Moorish Mayrit encompassed the area of the Alcázar and Almudena, and Mozárabe Matrice was situated by the area of Las Vistillas, both separated by the stream of San Pedro.

"Matrice" could be derived from the Latin term *matris* for "mother" or "principal", in reference to the San Pedro stream. It may also refer to the Manzanares River as being the "mother of waters".

Historian Jaime Oliver Asín dedicated over 400 pages to the research of the origins of the name of Madrid in his invaluable work, *Historia del Nombre "Madrid"*. Asín states that Mayrit was named after the abundance of *mayra* (qanat) or specific subterranean channels that were perfected in the area. It has often been said that the term "mayra", followed by the Iberro-Romance suffix "it", signifies a "place of" or "abundance of." Therefore "mayrit" can also be translated as "place with an abundance of subterranean water channels." This particular suffix is derived from the Latin equivalent of *etum* as we see in "Toletum" and "Mayoritum."

However, the curious reader may wonder why the Moors would name this new region after the abundance of water and add to it a Romance suffix rather than Arabic; yet the suffix *-it* does not exist in the Arabic language. Asín states that the Moors added the plural feminine Arabic suffix of *-at* to "mayra" (actually pronounced *-it*) meaning "a place of many Mayras." This etymology appears to make more sense. The origins of Madrid are Moorish; then so must be its name.

Another etymological theory suggests the name was derived from the Celtiberian term *Magerito* or *Mageterito* meaning "big ford", again related to water, as in a shallow area in a river or stream. Still others insist that its etymology is Celtiberian and is composed of the terms *magos* meaning "a field" and *rito*, meaning "a crossing."

Manzanares (Mantha-NAress): The name of the river that flows through Madrid has been explained as deriving from the Arabic *man nahar*, meaning "river of nourishment." However, as the Manzanares was known as the Guadarrama during Muslim rule, this etymological theory becomes questionable. The Castillian word for "apple" is *manzana* and the river may be named after the many apple orchards in the area.

Another theory states that it derives from *miaci nahar* or "river of Miaci", from *Miacum*, the urban settlement in Roman Madrid situated by the Manzanares River. The name of *Miacum* is said to originate from *miakud*, a Hebrew term related to fire. From here we derive the name of the stream from the Manzanares River known today as *Arroyo de Meaques* or "Meaques Stream" (pronounced *meh-ah-kes* in Castilian).

The humble Manzanares River was unable to provide sufficient water to the town due to the distance between the river and the plateau. Over the centuries, Madrid has been described as being a city without a river. Poet, playwright, and native of Madrid, Lope de Vega (1562–1635) wrote:

> ...*Manzanares claro,*
> *rio pequeño.*
> *Por faltarle el agua*
> *corre con fuego.*

> . . .The clear Manzanares,
> A small river.
> For lacking in water
> it flows with fire.

Maravedí: Between the 11th and 14th centuries, the Maravedí coin circulated throughout Spain. The Maravedí was originally set in gold and later was manufactured in silver. These coins were duplicated by Christian rulers of the 12th century and actually remained in use until 1854 when it was replaced by the *real*. The name is derived from the Arabic *Marabet* which was another form of the gold dinar that was struck for the first time in al-Andalus under the rule of Abd ar-Rahman III. This gold dinar or *Marabet* was named after the *al-Murabitun* or Almorávide Dynasty.

Marbella (Marbeya): The name of this picturesque town located in the province of Málaga in Andalusia translates as "pretty sea" in Castilian. This phrase is often cited as having been uttered by Queen Isabella when she first visited this town and said, "*Que mar tan bella!*" or "What a beautiful sea!" However, during Moorish rule, the town was already known as *Marbilha* or *Marbilya*

During Roman rule, Marbella was known as *Salduba*, "town of salt", as it was here where salt was manufactured. Salduba was founded as a strategic point where the Via Augusta passed.

In the year 1485, Caliph *Mohammed Abuenza* had no choice but to hand over the keys to the city to King Fernando. The end of Moorish Marbella is depicted in the Christian conquering scenes of Granada displayed upon the lower choir stalls of the Cathedral in Toledo. Today, you can still appreciate the ancient Muslim design of the historic quarter of Marbella and ruins of the Moorish walls and its towers.

Marbella Street

Mazapán (Matha-PAN): This delicious desert of marzipan was introduced to Spain by the Moors who knew it as *mawthaban*. Toledo is famous for their marzipan pieces that are shaped and sculpted into many curious shapes and forms such as animals and figures. The Castilian term may also be derived from the Latin *masa* meaning "pastry" and *panem* meaning "bread."

Marbella alcázar

Medina: The urban center of any Muslim city in known in Castilian as a Medina that derives from the Arabic *madinat* meaning "city." You can find this term integrated into several place names throughout Spain such as *Medina Sidonia* in Cádiz and *Salmedina* by the Manzanares, *Medinaceli* in Soria; *Medina Azahara* in Córdoba; *Medina de las Torres* in Badajoz; *Medina de Pomar* in Burgos; as well as *Medina de Rioseco* and *Medina del Campo*, both in Valladolid.

Mérida: This stronghold of the Roman Empire is situated in the province of Badajoz in west central Spain. Founded as *Colonia Augusta Emerita* by the Romans circa 25 BCE, Mérida was named after Emperor Augustus and the "emirates" or honored veteran soldiers that populated the colony. Prior to Toledo, Mérida was the capital of the Visigoth kingdom and during the 6th century, the Moors pronounced as *Meridah*.

Mijas (MEE-has): Around 600 ADE, this picturesque town located in the province of Málaga was founded by the Tartessians as *Tamisa*. Over the centuries the named evolved into *Mixa* and eventually into its present form. Mijas is also depicted in the Christian conquering scenes engraved upon the lower choir stalls of the Cathedral in Toledo.

Morisco: After the Reconquest, the Mudejares became known as Moriscos. These persecuted people were baptized and lived in Christian Spain until they were expelled from the country by Felipe III in 1610. "Morisco" is derived from the Latin *Mauri* or *Maurus*, the term used by the Romans for the dark-skinned inhabitants of the ancient Roman province of Mauritania.

Móstoles (MOS-toless): Situated 13 miles from Madrid, this suburb is believed to be named after a monastery that existed here during Roman times when it was known as *Monisterium*. Over the centuries, the name evolved into *Monsteriu*, *Moster*, and *Mostel* as it appeared documented in an Islamic travel chronicle.

The 13th century Mudejar tower of the church named *Iglesia de Nuestra Señora de la Asunción* in Móstoles is believed to have once been part of an Islamic atalaya or watchtower.

Motril: Situated on the Mediterranean coast in the province of Granada, Motril fell to the Christians in 1489 as illustrated in the conquering scenes engraved on the lower choir stalls of the Cathedral in Toledo. Its etymology consists of the Latin *murtetu* that signifies "place of myrtle" as many adorned the landscape of the area. When the Moors arrived they pronounced it as *Mutrayil*.

Mozárabe (Moh-THARabeh): A Christian of Visigoth ancestry living in Muslim Spain was known as a Mozárabe. This term is derived from the Arabic *must'arab* that roughly translates as "becoming an Arab." The Mozárabes had their own court and sometimes even held high positions within the Muslim courts. Interestingly, the Mozárabes did not refer to themselves by this name.

Mudéjar (Moo-DEHar): A Muslim that lived in Spain after the Reconquest, who was permitted to maintain his or her own property, religion, language, customs, and culture while paying a special tax, was known as a Mudéjar. The term, that first appeared documented in 1202, is derived from the Arabic *mudayyan* that translates as "allowed to stay." Exactly three hundred years later in 1502, the Mudéjars were given three months by the Catholic Kings to either leave their territory or convert to Christianity. Those who remained were well established, productive, and useful or profitable and were therefore bestowed certain honors and privileges. A large population of Muslims were expelled from Granada and settled in Madrid, particularly in the suburb of Getafe. As of the 16th century, the Mudéjars became known as *Moriscos* until they too were expelled from the country a century after.

Casa Lujanes

Mudéjar is also the name of the architectural style that this community developed. As of the 12th century, the Christians often employed Mudéjars in the construction of buildings as skilled architects or alarifes who excelled in architecture. The finest examples in Madrid of Mudéjar architecture is attributed to the towers on the churches of San Pedro and San Nicolás. The tower of San Nicolás stands as the oldest structure of Madrid and was declared a historic national monument in 1931. Another example of Mudéjar architecture can be appreciated at the house and tower of Los Lujanes at Plaza de la Villa that is dated to the 15th century. You will also find fine examples created by the Mudéjar alarifes in the nearby suburbs of Getafe, Mostoles, and Carabanchel.

Muladí (Moo-laDEE): A Mozárabe of Visigoth ancestry who converted to Islam during Moorish Spain in exchange for what was then a better life was known as a Muladí. The term is derived from the Arabic *muwalladín* being plural of *muwállad* that roughly translates as "not of an Arabic mother." The ancestry of a Muladí was diverse as one parent may have been a Muslim and the other a Christian.

The Muladíes spoke Arabic and practiced Muslim customs yet were regarded as inferior in status to the Arabs and Berbers. These people were suspiciously regarded by the Christians and never fully accepted by the Muslims.

Therefore, frequent disputes and rebellions arose as a result. Emir Muhammad I experienced many troubles at the hands of such Muladíes as *Ibn Marwan al-Yilliqi* whose ambition and bravery earned him the reputation of a rebel that led him to revolt against the Emir in 868. Al Yilliqi's great resistance and military efforts were rewarded as he surrendered and was given the title of Governor of Badajoz by the Emir himself in 875. Al-Yilliqi is considered by some as Andalusia's original bandit.

Umar ibn Hafsun was another notable Muladí of the 9th century. As a Muslim leader among Mozárabes and Muladíes, Hafsun led expeditions against the Umayyad Emirate of Córdoba. In the year 899, Hafsun of Visigoth ancestry, renounced Islam and was baptized receiving the Christian name of *Samuel*. A year before his death in 916, he switched sides joining forces with the Umayyads in a campaign against the northern Christian kingdoms.

The Basque-Muladí *Banu Qasi* Dynasty that ruled in the north during the 9th century is another example of prominent Muladíes, as was *Yusuf ibn Amrus* who functioned as governor of Toledo in 797 appointed by al-Hakam I, son of Abd ar-Rahman I.

Pamplona: Situated in north central Spain is the capital of Pamplona in the region of Navarre. Founded during the 1st century BCE by the Romans as *Pompaelo*, the town was named after Roman General *Pompey*. It is here where the famous spectacle known as the "running of the bulls" takes place every July in the streets of the old town. When the Moors arrived they pronounced it *Banbilunah* as the letter "p" is absent from the Arabic language.

Qadi (KAdee): In Moorish Spain, a judge or qadi was assigned to each of the major cities of al-Andalus; his duties were administrative as well as judicial. The Arabic term for "the judge" is *al-Qadi*, and from here we derive the Castilian word *alcalde* for "mayor."

Salamanca: Situated in west central Spain, Salamanca was founded by the Celtiberians or Greeks as *Helmantica*. The Romans named it *Salamantica*, possibly meaning "place near salt springs." Another version of its etymology, although doubtful, is that it is derived from the Greek *manta* that translates as "magic" or "divination" that was believed to have been taught here as a science.

The old historic quarter was declared a World Heritage Site by UNESCO in 1988. Salamanca is home to the oldest university in the country dated to 1218. It is also the name of one of the 21 districts belonging to Madrid that is considered as an expensive and upper class neighborhood.

Santiago de Compostela: As the capital of Galicia in northwest Spain, Santiago de Compostela is a significant Christian pilgrimage destination attracting over 175,000 visitors every year. The faithful not only arrive from the rest of Europe but from around the world as well. The pilgrimage route dates back to the 9th century and achieved major significance by the 12th century. After Jerusalem and Rome, Santiago de Compostela is considered to be the next most important Christian city in the world whose old town was named a World Heritage City in 1985. The name is composed of the Latin version of the apostle Saint James, "Santiago" and *Campus Stellae* that translates as "field of stars."

It is believed that it is here where the remains of Santiago were laid to rest. During the 1st century ADE, the apostle arrived in Spain to spread the gospel when he left the image of what was to be named the Virgin of Almudena. Upon returning to Judea, King Herod Agrippa had him beheaded in 44 ADE for not recruiting sufficient converts. For this reason Santiago was denied a proper burial and his remains were gathered by his devoted followers who transported them to Northern Spain.

According to legend, it was during the early 9th century when a local shepherd was guided by a beam of brilliant light from a star that shone upon a Roman necropolis. Upon further discovery, the shepherd found a small mausoleum buried among the dense vines, shrubs, and bushes. The shepherd came to the conclusion that the celestial star directed him to the burial place of the sacred remains. Another variation has the "shepherd" actually being Visigoth governor *Theodemir*, and yet another version is that the remains were discovered during the late 8th century by Charlemagne (Charles the Great), grandson of Charles Martel who halted the Muslim expansion into France and Europe.

The town"s Cathedral was built at the very spot in Galicia where his remains were supposedly found. Over the centuries, legends grew of visions and miracles that took place at Santiago de Compostela. Santiago, the Patron Saint of Spain, is also known in history as *Santiago Matamoros*, (Saint James the Moor-slayer), as it was believed that the image of Santiago appeared to the Christian soldiers, joining forces with them, as they fought in the victorious battles during the Reconquest.

Miguel de Cervantes writes of Saint James in *Don Quijote de la Mancha*:

> *Este si que es un caballero, y de las escuadras de Cristo: este se llama don San Diego Matamoros; uno de los más valientes santos y caballeros que tuvo el mundo y tiene ahora el cielo.*

> ...y mira que este gran caballero [Santiago] de la cruz bermeja háselo dado Dios a España por patrón y amparo suyo, especialmente en los rigurosos trances que con los moros los españoles han tenido, y así le invocan y llaman como defensor suyo en

todas las batallas que acometen, y muchas veces le han visto visiblemente en ellas derribando, atropellando, destruyendo y matando los agarenos escuadrones...

Now here is a nobleman, and of the squadrons of Christ: his name is Sir San Diego [Santiago] Matamoros, one of the most valiant saints and knights the world ever had who now belongs to the heavens.

...you see this great nobleman [Saint James] of the vermilion cross has been given by God to Spain as patron and protector, particularly because of the frequent extreme perils with the Spanish Moors, and so he is invoked and called upon in all the battles, and many times he has been seen knocking down, destroying and killing the Moorish squads...

Salobreña: Located in the Costa Tropical of Granada between Motril and Almuñécar, this lovely town was founded by the Phoenicians during the 13th century BCE as *Salambina*. The Phoenician etymology of its name can be broken down into *sal* or "salt" and *ambina* that translates as "around" or "in the region of", as a *salazón* or a fish-salting factory existed here. During the 2nd century BCE, Salobreña was known as *Segalvina* that the Moors later pronounced as *Salubiniya or Xalubina*.

Salobreña

Salobreña is a quaint white-washed town with a fine, wide beach that is split in half by a rock. The Arab castle sits high upon the town overlooking the Mediterranean, where spectacular views can be enjoyed. A fortification has existed at this very spot since the 10th century. Once serving as an inescapable prison, the military structure was built by the Christians during the late 15th century. The castle was declared a Cultural Heritage Monument by UNESCO in 1949. Salobreña was conquered by the Christians during the 15th century, as depicted in the lower choir stalls of the Cathedral in Toledo.

Alcázar of Salobreña

Segovia: Situated roughly 55 miles from Madrid, Segovia was known by the Romans during the 1st century BC as *Segubia* or *Secovia*. With a basic knowledge of Latin, one might suggest that it could derive from *seco* (dry or divided) and *via* (road or way). Some believe that its etymology is Celtic, *Segobriga*, derived from *sego*, meaning "victory" or "powerful", followed by the already-mentioned suffix of *-briga*. However, others insist that Segobriga was actually situated in the province of Cuenca. When the Moors arrived, they pronounced it as *Siqubiyyah*. Roman Segovia may have also been known as *Covia*, as this city is mentioned in Latin documents as housing a "wonderful aqueduct" that we can still appreciate today to the fullest.

In the enchanting town of Segovia, the most impressive Roman site can be admired in the form of a magnificent aqueduct that is dated between the 1st and 2nd century ADE. Situated in the center of the city, the aqueduct was used to bring water from the *Fuenfría Spring* or *Riofrío* (Cold River) that flowed from the mountains in the region of *Acebeda* about 12 miles away. This remarkable example of ancient architecture, still in use until the mid 20th century of our era, is comprised of 20,400 granite blocks and is nearly 98 feet in height. It is secured only by gravity; it was built without mortar or cement.

Still standing after two millennia, the structure is considered to be the best preserved example of Roman civil engineering in the world. Not surprisingly, in 1985 it was declared a World Heritage Site and in 1999 the American Society of Civil Engineers (ASCE) recognized the historical monument as an international landmark. This title has also been granted to the Eiffel Tower and the CN Tower, the Statue of Liberty, the Empire State Building, the Hoover Dam, as well as the Brooklyn and Golden Gate Bridges among others. Along with the aqueduct, the old town of Segovia itself was also declared a World Heritage City by UNESCO the same year. As with many local historical landmarks, this wondrous site also bears a legend:

During the days of Roman Spain, a young bewitching Segovian girl named *Juanilla* gathered water every morning from the fountains in the valley streams that she brought to her humble home. Growing increasingly tired from the long, arduous trek each day, Juanilla prayed for a solution to her problem. The devil heard her pleas and immediately appeared, proposing to build a spectacular aqueduct before the next sunrise that would bring water to her doorstep every morning that followed. However, in exchange for this great task, the enchanting girl's soul would be his for eternity. Clever Juanilla did not think such a great feat would be accomplished in such a short time, and so she agreed.

Juanilla stayed up all night and nervously watched as the aqueduct was rapidly approaching its completed state. She began to feverishly worry and switching faiths, Juanilla prayed to the Virgin Mary for a miracle and fell asleep.

The miracle was granted, as the sun rose earlier than expected. As a result, the devil did not have enough time to lay the final block of stone. Wise Juanilla not only gained a nearly completed aqueduct but managed to keep her soul intact as well. To this day, some say that the holes visible in the blocks of the aqueduct are the fingerprints of the devil himself, and for this reason it is also known as *Puente del Diablo* (Devil's Bridge).

The alcázar of Segovia, standing 200 feet upon a rocky cliff above the town, was once the favorite residence of Castilian rulers. The structure served as the royal residence of Queen Isabella I and it was here where a historic meeting took place between the Queen and Christopher Columbus as they discussed the funding of his future milestone expedition. When the court was moved to Madrid, the Alcázar was used as a prison. The Alcázar, although built over Roman ruins, has been completely rebuilt several times. Its present form however, is dated to the mid 19th century. It is believed to have been the inspiration behind Walt Disney's fairy tale castles.

Segovia Alcázar

The Cathedral of Segovia is regarded as the last Gothic cathedral to be constructed in the country. It was at this very spot in the main plaza where the Cathedral was later built that Isabella was proclaimed Queen of Castile. Although construction began during the 16th century, it was not completed until just after the mid 18th century.

Segovia Cathedral

Simancas: In the province of Valladolid, Simancas was known as *Septimanca* during Roman Spain. While its origins are Celtiberian, the town is believed to have been named by the Romans after the *séptima via romana* or "seventh Roman road" that traveled from Mérida to Zaragoza where it was situated. When the Moors arrived they pronounced it as *Shant Mankash.* It was here where the three-day battle took place in the summer of 939 when Ramiro II of León defeated the Muslims., although Abd ar-Rahman III narrowly escaped with his own life, he lost over 50,000 of his men. A subway station in the metro of Madrid is named after this historic town.

Tajo (TAho): The longest river within the Iberian Peninsula is the Rio Tajo. The Tagus River, as it is known in English, flows from the *Albarracín Mountains* east of Madrid to southwest into the Atlantic Ocean at Lisbon, Portugal. Its name is derived from the Latin *Tagus* and Ancient Greek *Tagos*; both meaning "to cut through."

Talamanca: Muhammad I founded this defensive site during the 9th century as *Talamankah*, a permutation of "Talavera" and "Salamanca." The origins of the name are Celtiberian and could be translated as "place near a hill" or "place near a watchtower" as the Arabic *tal* means "hill" and *tala'i* translates as "watchtower." Today it is known as *Talamanca de Jarama* for its proximity to the Jarama River.

Talavera: Located in Toledo, Talavera was founded by the Celts as *Talabriga* and renamed by the Romans as *Caesarobriga*. Historian *Titus Livius* (59 – 17 ADE) refers to Talavera as *Aebura*. Another theory is that its origins are Moorish; as it was known in al-Andalus as *Talabira* that is derived from *tal al-abira* meaning "the hill of the river bank" or "hill on the shore." Muslim chronicles state that Musa ibn Nusayr joined Tariq ibn Ziyad here in 712. Ali ibn Yusuf took Talabira during the early 12th century when he destroyed most of Mayrit. Today it is known as *Talavera de la Reina* (Talavera of the Queen), this appellation was added by King Alfonso XI when he presented the town to his wife as a dowry during the 14th century.

Tánger (TANher): Tangier, on the western side of the Mountains in Northern Morroco, was known as *Tingis* during Roman rule although its origins are Phoenician. Its etymology is also related to Berber and Greek mythology; *Sufax*, the grandson of Poseidon, God of the Sea, was said to have been the founder of Tangier who named it after his mother *Tinjis*. However, the most acceptable theory is that the term is derived from the Berber term *tingis*, meaning "marsh" that is plentiful in the area.

Tangier has its place in the history of al-Andalus. It is here where the Governor of Ceuta, Count Julian, asked the Governor of Tangier, Tariq ibn Ziyad, for assistance in dethroning the Visigoths. In the year 711, Tariq left Tangier and disembarked with his army of men at Gibraltar opening the door to Muslim rule in Spain and Portugal for centuries to come. Governor and General Musa Ibn Nusayr, who also led a successful expedition to the peninsula a year after, was the first Muslim to occupy Tangier. *Tanja*, as it is known in Arabic, is the capital of the Tánger-Tetuán region of Northern Morroco.

Tangiers

Tetuán (Teh-TWAN): Located in northern Morocco, Tetuán is considered to be the most Andalusian city of Morocco. Its name is derived from either *Titawan*, meaning "eyes" in Berber or "springs" in Arabic. In Madrid, you will find a street, an underground metro station, and a district named Tetuán. This predominantly Muslim district is where the second largest mosque of Madrid is situated, built over a site of a former Visigoth necropolis. The neighbourhood of Tetuán was named after the North African city as a result of the Spanish victory in the Battle of Tetuán of 1860 during the Spanish-Moroccan Wars. In this battle, the soldiers set up camp at a northern area of Madrid that became known as *Tetuán de las Victories* (Tetuán of the Victories.)

Tetuan

Further battles took place between Spain and the Berber *Rif* tribe of Northern Morocco that resulted in the First Rif War of 1893. In 1909 another battle followed known as the Second Rif War that resulted in the death of a few Spanish miners after receiving no support from Madrid when requested by the military commander of Melilla in Morocco. It is reported that the Spanish victory was achieved at the cost of the lives of over 2,500 of their own men.

Rif Soldier

In the Treaty of Fez of 1912, Spain was given what are known as the Spanish enclaves in Northern Africa of Ceuta and Melilla. In 1920, the Third Rif War took place resulting in the victory of the Spaniards and French over the Rif tribe, where tens of thousands of soldiers died on both sides.

Titulcia (Tee-TOOLtheeyah): As an important settlement along the way between Mérida and Zaragoza, Titulcia may have been known as *Titulcium* during Roman Spain, possibly deriving from the

Latin *titulus* meaning "title." In Celtiberian, it has been translated as "the way" or "the path." Another theory is that Titulcia may have been named after the Roman Emperor *Titus Flavius* of the 1st century ADE.

Toledo: The Celtiberians founded Toledo as *Toletum*, a name that persisted during Roman Spain that translates as "elevated." The name of Toletum first appears in the writings of 1st century ADE Roman historian Titus Livius. Another etymological theory is that Jewish colonists are believed to have founded Toledo in the year 450 BCE as *Toledoth* that translates as "mother of people" or "generations." Another similar version has the Jewish refugees from Jerusalem founding Toledo as *Tolaitola* that comes from the Hebrew word *tolatola* possibly meaning "exile." During Moorish rule, it was known as *Tulaytulah.*

Valencia (VaLEN-theeya): Situated about 220 miles to the east of Madrid, this town was known by the Romans as *Valentia Edetanorum*, that translates as "power" and named after the *Edetani* who were an Iberian tribe from Northern Spain that settled along the Ebro Valley. When the Moors arrived they pronounced it as *Balansiyya.*

Valencia was conquered in 1090 by the Mozárabe military hero and conqueror El Cid Campeador. Born Rodrigo Díaz de Vivar, El Cid fought for both the Muslims and the Christians, but ultimately joined the Christian side. In 1094 he was appointed ruler of Valencia on behalf Alfonso VI. This important figure in the history of Spain is believed to have halted the Islamic invasion of Western Europe and helped paved the way for the complete Christianization of the Iberian Peninsula.

Valencia is known as the home of Spain's traditional seafood and rice dish known as *paella* and it is here that the best can be sampled. *Horchata* is the name of a popular drink made of tiger nuts, sugar, and water that also originated in Valencia during Muslim rule. This milky beverage comes with an interesting and highly questionable yet amusing folk etymology:

After the conquest of Valencia, King Juan I of Aragón was served a glass of this milky beverage by a young Arab girl and apparently enjoyed the drink so much that upon tasting Horchata for the first time exclaimed, "¡Aixo es or, xata!" translated in Castilian as "¡Eso es oro, chata!" meaning, "This is gold, sweetie!"

Valladolid (Vaya-doLEED): Situated roughly 105 miles northwest from Madrid, Valladolid is believed to have been founded by the Celts as *Vallis Toletum* that translates as "elevated valley." Valladolid was known by the Moors as *Balad al-Walid*, that translates as "town of *al-Walid*" possibly named after the Caliph *Al-Walid ibn Abd al-Malik* of the Umayyad Dynasty who ruled during the early 8th century.

It was in Valladolid where the Catholic Monarchs, Isabella and Fernando, were betrothed in 1469, joining their lives and two kingdoms as one. It was also here where Christopher Columbus took his last breath in 1506. Valladolid was the capital of Spain until it was replaced by Madrid in 1561 by Felipe II until Felipe III made Valladolid once again the capital of the country between 1600 and 1606. Felipe IV was born in Valladolid in 1605. It is said that in Valladolid particularly and Salamanca is where the best Castilian in the country is spoken.

Valmardón: The name of this 10th century gate in Toledo is a corruption of the name of the nearby mosque of *Bab al-Mardum* that translates as "Gate of the People" in Arabic. Since the Reconquest, the former mosque has been known as *El Cristo de La Luz* (Christ of the Light) and is presently open to visitors.

Valnadú: Also referred to but less frequently as *Balnadú*, this is the name of one of the four gates of Madrid's Christian wall. *Valnadú* is actually a corruption of the *Bab an-Nadur* that translates in Arabic as "gate of the watchtowers" from the root verb *nadara* meaning "to look" and *bab* meaning a "gate" or "door." Another possible etymology includes the Latin *balnea* meaning "bath house" and *duo* meaning "two" as bath houses were located nearby.

To speculate on its etymology, it could very well be derived from the Latin *valle* or *vallis* meaning "valley" as it faced the northern valley, and *nadu* or *natus* meaning "to be born" or "to spring forth" that can be translated as "gate where the valley springs forth."

Zamora (Tha-Mora): Situated near the border of Portugal, Zamora is believed to have been the Roman *Ocelum Duri* or "eyes of the Duero River", as it is referred to in the "Itinerary of Antonino." It was eventually shortened to *cemuri* (pronounced "themooree") and evolved from there into its present name. During the 6th century, the city appears as the Visigoth *Semure* that may have evolved into the Arabic *Az-Zemur* during Moorish rule.

Zarzuelas (Thar-THWEH-las): The operettas or musical plays that developed in Madrid during the 17th century are known as Zarzuelas. This musical opera was named after the royal hunting lodge of Palacio de la Zarzuela where the first operetta was performed for court members and royalty. The term is derived from *zarza*, meaning "blackberries", as as many were found here in the remote countryside. Other sources have this term meaning "thorny bush" or "shrub" derived from the Arabic *sharas*. The *zarza* produces a type of blackberry or *mora* that in Castilian is also known as a *zarzamora*.

Zocodover (Thocodo-VER): The popular town square or plaza in the heart of Toledo is known as Plaza de Zocodover. Its etymology is Arabic deriving from *sûq* or "market" and *ad-dawab* meaning "the livestock" as it was here where a cattle marketplace was located during the middle of the 15th century. Today, the triangular and busy square is considered as the central or meeting point of the city and is within walking distance to all the main historic sites.

10. CLOSING

Medina Mayrit, often described as a small military hill town, was exclusively built to stop the advances of Christian troops from the north and to protect the ruling Umayyad Dynasty. Mayrit started as a modest but well-defended fortress; however, the battles to conquer it, led by Ramiro II in 932 and in 950, accompanied by Fernán González, as well as Alfonso VI in 1085, show the relative importance of this once small settlement. Although the Moors were not the first to occupy the area, they are the official founders of the city. It is one of the few cities of al-Andalus that was built entirely by the Moors as most were raised over former Roman or Visigoth villages.

Mayrit did not reach the great heights that such cities as Toledo and Córdoba achieved, but nevertheless grew from a simple Almudena into a Medina and just a few centuries later, becoming the capital of the Kingdom of Spain. Moorish Madrid did not evolve into a major center of trade or commerce; however it maintained its character as an outstanding military fort. Excelling in agricultural methods as well, Mayrit was praised throughout al-Andalus for possessing an abundance of vineyards, orchards, farmlands, groves, and pastures. The art and technique of producing fine ceramics and pottery-making created with various different techniques and forms further added to the uniqueness of Mayrit.

However, in addition to its military and agricultural disposition, we can say that Medina Mayrit was best known in al-Andalus for its subterranean canals introduced by the Moors that provided water to the settlement. Although, the richness of the land existed before they arrived, the Moors were the first to apply ingenious methods in obtaining and chanelling water specifically in Mayrit.

As traces of the Moors have nearly vanished, one can still appreciate the structure of Moorish Madrid with its narrow and windings streets and typical Muslim style plazas of the historic quarter of the old Morería. There are but a few names of streets and plazas that echo the distant voice of Moorish Madrid such as Puerta de Moros, Plaza del Arrabal, Plaza del Alamillo, Alameda, and Almudena, and Morería.

Calle de la Morería

From the Greek *Mantua*, Roman *Miacum*, and Visigoth *Matrice* to Moorish *Mayrit*, Madrid today possesses a strong and lively character blended with a visual beauty, incorporating modern and classical elements such as historical landmarks and picturesque buildings that color the city's appearance and disposition. I am proud to say that my birthplace is rightfully considered one of the most beautiful capitals of Europe today.

Bibliography

al-Makkari, Ahmed ibn Mohammed. *The History of the Mohammedan Dynasties in Spain.* London, England; Routledge Curzon, 2002.

Asin Oliver, Jaime. *Historia del Nombre "Madrid".* Madrid, Spain; agencia Española de Cooperación Internacional, 1991

Aulestia, Gorka, et al. *Basque-English, English-Basque Dictionary.* Nevada, US; University of Nevada Press, 1992.

Cadalso, José. *Cartas Marruecas.* Barcelona, Spain; Salvat Editores, 1970.

Capilla, Susana Calvo. *Urbanismo en La Córdoba Islámica.* Madrid, Spain; Edilupa Ediciones, 2002.

de Cervantes, Miguel. *Don Quijote de la Mancha.* Valladolid, Spain; Ediciones Castilla, 1967.

Christys, Ann. *Christians in Al-Andalus, 711-1000.* Surrey, England; Curzon Press, 2002.

Cortes y Lopez, Don Miguel. *Diccionario Geografico-Historico de la Espana Antigua.* Madrid, Spain; Imprenta Real, 1836

da Cunha Bermejo, Jose Antonio. *El Reino Visigodo de Toledo.* Toledo, Spain; Ediciones Covarrubias, 2007

Díaz, José Simón. *Guía Literiaria de Madrid; Arrabales y Barrios Bajos.* Madrid, Spain, Ediciones La Librería, 1994.

Díaz, José Simón. *Guía Literiaria de Madrid; De Murallas Adentro.* Madrid, Spain, Ediciones La Librería, 1993.

García de Cortázar, Fernando. *Historia de España.* Barcelona, Spain; Editorial Planeta, 2003.

Gea Ortigas, Isabel. *Las Murallas de Madrid*. Madrid, Spain; Ediciones La Librería, 1999

Gea Ortigas, Isabel and Oñate Castellanos, Jose Manuel. *Madrid Musulmán, Judío y Cristiano; Las Murallas Medievales de Madrid*. Madrid, Spain; Ediciones La Librería, 2008.

González-Ruano, César. *Madrid*. Barcelona, Spain; Editorial Noguer, 1963.

Hernández Girbal, F. *Bandidos Celebres Españoles (en la Historia y en la Leyenda.)* Madrid, Spain; Edicioines Lira, 1993.

Imamuddin, S.M. *Muslim Spain 711-1492 A.D.* Leiden, Netherlands; E.J. Brill, 1981.

Kurlansky, Mark. *The Basque History of the World*. Toronto, Canada; Vintage Canada, 2001.

Jiménez, Jorge. *El Mudéjar Madrileño*. Madrid, Spain; Ediciones La Librería, 2001.

Lopez Gomez, Antonio. *Madrid desde la Academia*. Madrid, Spain; Real Academia de la Historia, 2001.

Madriaga, Antonio Méndez, et al. *Madrid del Siglo IX al XI*. Madrid, Spain; Real Academia de Bellas Artes de San Fernando, 1990

Marín Guzmán, Roberto. *Sociedad, Política y Protesta Popular en la España Musulmana*. San Jose, Costa Rica; Editorial Universidad de Costa Rica, 2006.

Martínez Sanz, José Luis. *Al-Andalus; Los Árabes en España*. Madrid, Spain; Edimat Libros, 2007.

Montero Vallejo, Manuel. *El Madrid Medieval*. Madrid, Spain; Ediciones La Librería, 2003.

Montero Vallejo, Manuel. *Madrid Musulmán, Cristiano y Bajo Medieval*. Madrid, Spain; Editorial El Avapiés, 1990.

Montoliú Camps, Pedro. *Madrid Villa y Corte*. Madrid, Spain; Silex Ediciones, 1996.

Peña Marcos, José María. *Al-Andalus: 711-756*. Madrid, Spain; Editorial Visión Libros, 2005.

Ramos, Rosalia and Revilla, Fidel. *Madrid Medieval*. Madrid, Spainl Ediciones La Librería, 2003.

Reilly, Bernard F. *The Medieval Spains*. Cambridge, UK; Cambridge University Press, 1993.

de Répide, Pedro. *Las Calles de Madrid*. Barcelona, Spain; Kaydeda Ediciones, 1989.

Salas Vázuez, Eduardo. *Testimonios del Madrid Medieval; El Madrid Musulmán*. Madrid, Spain; Museo de San Isidro, 2002.

Sepúlveda, Ricardo and Comba, Juan. *Costumbres, Leyendas y Descripciones de la Villa y Corte en los Siglos Pasados; Madrid Viejo*. Madrid, Spain; Librería de Fernando Fé, 1887.

Vives, Jaime Vicens. Aproximación a la Historia de Espana. Barcelona, Spain; Salvat Editorial, 1970.

Watt, W. Montgomery. *Historia de la España islámica.* Madrid, Spain; Alianza Editorial, 1970.

INDEX